The Final Days of the United States

And How You Can Survive Them

Charles Bennett

FOREWARD

2016 was one of the worst years ever in the United States of America. And not just as it relates to the presidential election.

The whole process brought forth the sheer ugliness that mankind has to offer.

Hidden biases were exposed. As were the shameless ways campaigns conducted their operations.

The Republican National Committee was caught red-handed supporting its favored candidates over an outsider.

Democrats gloated gleefully, but not for long.

Just weeks later the Democratic National Committee was busted for doing exactly the same thing.

Heads rolled. Fingers were pointed. Lies were told.

And then it got even uglier.

All semblance of civility was thrown out the window.

The name calling commenced. Mud-slinging led to all-out slander.

And grown men and women began behaving like four-year olds to adoring crowds.

Who apparently liked it.

The country was almost evenly divided. And whichever side was losing at any given time claimed the country was walking straight off a cliff.

These are dark days for the United States of America. She has lost her status as the greatest country on earth. She's now ridiculed instead of admired, and her best days are behind her.

She's tottering on the brink of bankruptcy and making more and more enemies by the day.

Enemies who are toying with the idea of demanding payment on their loans.

Enemies who have the capability of collapsing the almighty dollar with the stroke of a pen.

It's just a matter of time. Perhaps years.

Or perhaps days.

Whenever it does happen, the dollar will be worthless.

And the once-mighty United States of America will fall like a house of cards.

Only those who make preparations beforehand have a chance of survival.

You've seen the prepper shows on all the cable channels. They prepare for a variety of catastrophes, from electromagnetic pulses to nuclear fallout.

Few of them prepare for economic collapse. And let's face it. In the state the United States is now in, that's the only realistic scenario.

In fact, it's not only a realistic scenario.

It's inevitable. It's just a matter of time.

We need to prepare, and the sooner the better.

But let's face it. Most of these shows center around multi-millionaires who have the money to purchase an old missile silo in the prairies of North Dakota somewhere. Or the guy who has a 400 acre ranch in Colorado. Or the guy with so much money in the bank that he can build a house with four foot-thick reinforced walls and bullet and bomb-proof windows.

Or the guy who thinks he can just buy his way out of trouble, and hoards half a million dollars worth of gold bouillon to trade for water and bullets and food, and whatever else he needs.

I don't know about you guys, but I don't have millions of dollars to buy an old missile silo, or to hoard gold. I've never even been on a 400 acre ranch, and I couldn't even make a down payment on a bullet and bomb-proof house.

Me, I'm just an ordinary guy. I live in the suburbs. In a housing development, in a regular house.

And I'm just guessing now, but I'll bet most of you are more like me than you are like the missile silo guy. And that's the purpose behind this book.

I've been prepping for years. I've experimented with food preparation and storage, various low cost security methods, and various ways to help my family survive whatever ugliness is coming our way.

I can help you with things like sanitizing your water supplies safely, without wasting big money on fancy filtration systems. How to build an outhouse for around a hundred dollars. How to protect your back yard from prowlers without any fancy alarm systems. How to hide in plain sight. And a bunch of other things that'll help you survive when the cities go black and the rest of the world starts to panic.

By the way, I'm no big famous writer who uses fancy words to impress people. I write like I speak. I think that's the best way to make myself understood. I've been told that for most people, it's the most comfortable way for them to read a book.

And let's face it. You didn't buy this book so I could impress you with my vocabulary. You bought this book so I could help you survive. So let's get started.

Table of Contents

1.
Hiding in Plain Sight

Securing your home is the first critical step in surviving. You'll have preppers who spend all their time focusing on gathering food. Other preppers will gather as much water as they can. Others will collect supplies.

But all of them, every last one, will be wasting their time if they don't secure their homes. Because when their neighbors who didn't make any preparations to hoard water or food start to run out, they'll be coming. And the first places they'll hit are those who are most vulnerable.

Because security is the cornerstone of your survival, that's what we'll talk about first. The first few chapters will give you some common sense and low cost means for protecting your family and your property from those who think it's easier to steal from someone else than to make their own preparations.

Okay, we'll start with what I call hiding in plain sight. More specifically, convincing marauders that your house is vacant. This is the single most important thing you can do to protect yourself when Armageddon arrives. It's something you cannot do ahead of time. However, you need to go over the process in your own mind and with those on your team, so it can be done quickly and efficiently when the time is right.

Why hide in plain sight, you ask? Because when the power grid goes down, or the economy collapses, or any one of a dozen other scenarios play out in the form of a disaster, most people will be unprepared. They won't have the things they need to survive. And they'll have to resort to stealing what they need.

When they come, they'll come looking for houses with people in them. Vacant houses are of no use to them. So… you have to convince them that your house is vacant.

The first thing I want you to do is go on the internet and Google "Foreclosure Notice." What you're looking for is a form letter that banks post on front doors when they kick people out of their homes. There are several versions where you just fill in the blanks. You can buy one of them for a dollar or two, or make your own on your computer. If you make your own, though, you've got to do a good enough job to make it look official. The people who come around to steal your food may not be too bright, but even some of them might notice if you misspell "eviction."

Anyway, you'll need three copies of the eviction notice. Fill them out the same way. Make it appear that your bank repossessed your house a few days before. Be sure it has dates on it and a phony bank manager's signature on the bottom. The more official it looks, the more likely the marauders and looters will bypass your house and go to somebody else's.

On the day the stuff hits the fan and panic is sweeping the earth, you'll be a busy guy. So will everybody else on your team. Because there's a lot to be done.

The next thing you need to do is hang the foreclosure notices. One on your front door. One on that big picture window in the front of the house, and the third one smack in the center of your garage door.

The one in the window needs to go on the inside. If you can protect the other two with a plastic protector of some type, do so. They'll last longer. If you can't, then tape it up real good so the rain doesn't destroy it and it doesn't blow away.

But that's just the first step.

The next step is to clear that front room. You remember, the one with the big picture window? Get all the furniture out of there. Everything. Get everything off the walls. Get the curtains and drapes off the windows.

Then raise the blinds all the way up.

If a looter looks into your front window, you want him to see the empty room and think the whole house is that way.

So if there are any hallways or anything else you can see from the front window, they'll have to be sanitized also.

You can do this in one of two ways. The first option is to simply strip the hallway like you did the front room. If that's not an option for whatever reason, your next bet is to place a door there. It doesn't matter if there was never a door there before. All you have to do is pull the hinge pins from one of the bedroom doors somewhere else in the house and tack it into place between the front room and the hallway. The lights will always be off in that room, so it'll be semi-dark even in the daytime. The looter will look into your window, see that the front room is empty. If he can see up the hallways, he'll see that they're empty too. If he can't see the hallway because there's a door in the way, he'll assume the door leads to a master bath or closet. Either way, he'll think the house is empty and he'll go to another one.

But wait… there's more work to do.

If your house has a second story, you must prepare it as well. Remove the curtains and drapes, and close the blinds to within a quarter of an inch, so that you can see out, but no one can see in. If there are no blinds on the window, cover it with black plastic and cut a 3/8 inch peephole into it.

Do the same thing to any window that can be seen from the street, so that no one standing in the yard or in the street in front of your house can see inside the windows.

If you can get by without the upstairs rooms that face the street, then do it. Just close the doors to those rooms and tell everybody to stay the hell out of there, except for your sentries pulling guard duty.

But wait. You're not finished yet.

You still have the front yard to deal with.

All patio furniture, planters, etc, must go. If you have a few rolled up newspapers, throw them in the garage now and save them just for this purpose. When the time comes, put them on the front porch. The cars in the driveway will either have to go in the garage or down the street.

When you're finished, if you do it correctly, the house will appear totally empty. And nobody steals food and water from an empty house.

A couple of things to remember…

I'm going under the assumption that your house has a six foot tall wooden privacy fence that is most common in the suburbs these days. If it does, check the spaces between the slats. Some fence installers make the spaces too wide to save on wood, and you can see people moving around behind the fence.

If that's the case with your fence, you have two options. You can cordon off the areas in your back yard where you might be visible from the street.

Or, if you need your whole back yard to grow crops (more on that in a later chapter), then a cheap twenty dollar plastic tarp, nailed to the inside of your fence, prevent looters and marauders from seeing movement between your fence slats.

If you have a six foot block wall, you're covered. If you have a lower fence, you're limited to option one: cordon off any area in the back yard where you might be visible from the front yard. And stay out of those areas.

One last note about hiding in plain sight. This almost goes without saying, but I'll mention it anyway. No candles or flashlights in the front rooms of the house after dark. None. Nada. Zilch. All it takes is one slip-up to announce your presence to the whole neighborhood.

2.
Fortifying Your Back Yard

Okay, you've made ourselves invisible to the neighborhood by making your house look like it's vacant.

Now we're going to take the next step. We're going to fortify the back yard.

Relax. I know you're on a budget. So am I. This is only going to cost you about thirty to forty dollars, depending on the size of your back yard. And it's highly effective in keeping prowlers and looters out of your yard.

This requires a little bit of prep work before the apocalypse arrives. But not much. I prepped my back yard in about three hours. But then. I'm pretty fast with a drill.

Okay, here's what you need: an electric drill, which you probably already have in your garage; and a couple of boxes of inch and a quarter wood screws.

Exactly how many screws you'll need depends on how big your yard is. Go completely around your yard and count the number of fence pickets you have. The fence pickets are those six foot tall slats that are nailed to the fence's three horizontal cross pieces.

The most common type of picket is a six inch dog-ear, so that's the kind we'll discuss here.

(Chances are you have the six inch dog-ear, but if you don't, you'll have something very similar. Just modify these instructions the best you can and you're good to go).

The six inch dog ear got its name because it's not completely flat across the top. It's been trimmed on each side, so that the flat top of the picket is actually only four inches wide.

Take your electric drill and drill two holes on the top of each of the slats, about an inch or so below the top of the slat. Buy your screws first, before you select your drill bit. Select a bit that will accommodate the screw snugly, but not too tight. This part is important, and we'll explain why in a minute.

Go completely around the yard. Two holes in each slat, one inch from the top of the fence.

Once you're done, you'll have a choice to make.

You can either fortify your fence now, by screwing in the screws so that the points face the outside of your yard. If you fortify it now, it's guaranteed to keep out prowlers even now, before the world goes black. And let's face it, in the world we live in today, that might not be a bad idea.

Except...

There have been two occasions in the last year when I've have to climb over my own fence because I left my keys in the house and the door latched behind me. And I tore the hell out of my arms and legs getting over the damn thing.

So it's an individual choice. Base it on your own situation.

If you choose not to fortify your fence now, then just put the screws on a shelf in the garage and wait for the day when the stuff hits the fan. When you need them, the holes will be pre-drilled, and the screws can go into the holes in no time at all.

Remember a few paragraphs back when I told you to make the drill holes snug, but not too tight?

Here's why.

We don't know what's going to happen in the future that will make you fortify your house and take shelter in it. Scientists and preppers have been debating for years about what kind of catastrophe will cause that to happen.

It could be something as simple as the collapse of the economy, and the starvation and rioting that ensues.

It could be something more sinister, like a terrorist group that gets its hand on dirty bombs. Or, even worse, real nukes.

My personal feeling is that we're long overdue for solar storms of such magnitude that they'll bombard the earth with electromagnetic pulses (EMPs). When that happens, the EMPs will be so powerful that anything electric or electronic will be instantly and permanently shorted out. (There are some steps to take to protect a limited amount of electronics, but it's a pain in the ass. More on that later)

There is scientific evidence that solar storms in the early 1800s resulted in a flurry of EMPs striking the earth. A lot of cattle got dizzy and fell over, and some people fainted and got nauseated. It didn't do any damage, though, because back then there were no machines or electronics. Scientists believe that sunspot activity, like most other things in the universe, run in cycles. And that we're due another batch of EMPs any time now.

If you want to know more about EMPs, go on Amazon.com and get a copy of *"Countdown to*

Armageddon," by Darrell Maloney. It's a novel about EMPs zapping the earth and ways to prepare for it. It's $2.99, but well worth three bucks.

Then again, some believe a huge volcanic eruption or meteorite collision will kick up such a dirt cloud that the sun will be hidden for years and that the world will freeze.

The point is, we don't know what's going to happen the day the earth goes dark. But under many scenarios, you may not have electricity. Electric drills would be worthless at that point, and we don't want you to be spending hours and hours in your back yard trying to install screws into the holes in your fence with a manual screwdriver, if the holes are too tight for them.

That's why the best option is snug, but not too tight.

By the way, this is a perfect job if you have teenagers, or for the women in your group to do. It's monotonous and important, but doesn't require a lot of skill. And you can be doing other stuff, like getting the cars out of your driveway and moving furniture out of your front room and such, while others are fortifying your fence.

Whether you fortify your fence now, or when doomsday comes, the end result will be the same. From the outside of the fence, intruders will be forced to climb over a fence topped with sharp screws placed three inches across, the entire top of the fence. As I said, I've had to climb over my own fence twice in the last year.

I can personally testify that it's impossible to climb over such a fence without ripping your hands, arms and legs to shreds. Not to mention a thirty dollar pair of Wranglers. That's what hurt the most.

Okay, cost of this project:

It cost me $22. I already had the drill and the bits, so all I had to buy was the screws. I waited until Home Depot had them on sale and bought them then. And they even gave me a discount for being a military retiree (USMC, Semper Fi).

It's a good idea to buy more screws than what you need, if you're not sure. The reason why is because we'll talk about several other projects you can undertake in later chapters.

And let's face it, we're guys. We can never have too many tools, hardware or Hooters calendars, right?

3.
Building an Outhouse for About $100

Okay, on to a totally different kind of project.

Let's talk about my second favorite subject in the whole wide world: outhouses.

That's right. Something we don't like to think about ever having to use. Much less having to build. But you'll be amazed at how easy they are.

First, a list of what you'll need…

If you've ever installed a fence or replaced a broken fence post, you'll know what post hole diggers are. If you don't know, it's simply a digging device that has two small shovels attached to long handles. The shovels pivot in a scissor-like manner when the handles are separated, to scoop dirt out of the ground. They're located in the garden section for around $30 or so.

But don't buy any if you can help it. Post hole diggers are like wheelbarrows and fertilizer spreaders. You seldom need them, and mostly they just get in the way in your garage. So if you have a neighbor who owns a set, just borrow his instead.

If you do borrow your neighbor's set, read this book completely through first. I'll talk about other projects later on that will also require post hole diggers. You might consider deciding which projects you'll want to undertake now, and pre-dig all your post holes. You can always fill them back in with loose dirt, and you'll be able to easily dig them out later even if the post hole diggers aren't available then.

You'll need a few other things as well. Two fence posts. The 4" by 4" by 6' size will do fine.

And three two by fours, eight feet long. And fifteen fence pickets, like the ones your fence is already made of. You'll need a drill so you can pre-drill the holes, and you'll need some 1 ¼ inch screws. Maybe a hundred or so. If you have that many left over from when you fortified your fence, you can just use them. You'll need four 2 inch "L" brackets (like the ones for your roof gutter system), and a piece of scrap plywood three feet by two feet. Lastly, you'll need fifteen landscaping bricks, like the ones in the photo below. Walmart sells the bricks for about three bucks apiece. Home Depot sometimes has them on sale for less than that. And three bags of Sacrete (premixed concrete. $2.65 a bag at Home Depot).

Total cost of your outhouse: Around $100. Not bad, huh?

Okay, next we'll talk about where you're going to place it. Because of the smell factor, you're going to want to put it as far away from the house as possible. Also, this will be an open top outhouse, also because of the smell factor. Since it'll have no roof, you'll want it far enough away from the house to give yourself some privacy. You don't want to be sitting in the outhouse, doing your business and reading an old copy of Sports Illustrated, and look up to see your sentry waving at you from the upstairs window. That's why we're going to put it in the back corner of your yard instead of by the back door.

Virtually all fences in the suburbs these days have six foot tall privacy fences. So that's what we're going to focus on. If you don't have a six foot privacy fence, modify these plans as best you can.

Here's how to build your hundred dollar outhouse:

1. Eighteen inches from your back fence, and eighteen inches from your side fence, use the post hole diggers to dig a hole. You could use a shovel, but with post hole diggers you can go much deeper without collapsing the sides. And you want a clean hole. Make it twelve inches wide and four feet deep.

2. Now dig a post hole flush up against your back fence, and exactly three feet away from the side fence.

3. Once that's done, run a tape measure and mark your next hole. Measured from the center of one hole to the center of the next hole, you'll want the holes to be exactly eight feet apart, and running parallel to your side fence.

4. Dig each hole about twenty four inches deep. Put the post holes in the holes, make sure they're straight, and pour a bag and a half of Sacrete into each hole. Don't worry about mixing it in a tub and all that stuff. It'll hold this way, I promise, and this way is much easier.

5. One each post is straight, brace it so it doesn't move when the Sacrete settles. Then fill the hole with water, up to the top of the hole. The Sacrete will absorb the water and any excess will soak into the dirt surrounding the hole.

5. Leave the posts to dry for at least 36 hours. Then go back and place the three two by fours horizontally between the posts. Use the existing fence as a guide to show you where to place them. Basically, the lower brace should be about twelve inches or so off the ground. The top one should be flush with the tops of the two posts. The center brace should be… well, centered. Be sure you mount the braces on the outside of the outhouse, not the inside.

6. Then put the pickets up. They'll go the full length of the braces. All eight feet of them. You might ask, "But they're only six inches wide. Won't I need sixteen instead of fifteen?" The answer is no. You need to leave a slight gap between each picket, to allow room for swelling and warpage. If you don't, the pickets may buckle later on and fall off. And if that happens, it'll happen at the worst possible time, like when you're sitting there taking a crap and all the kids are playing in the yard.

7. Now step back and take a look. You should have a three-sided enclosure, eight feet long and three feet wide, with a deep hole in the back. If you have anything other than that, go back to step number one and figure out what went wrong.

8. Put your first layer of five landscaping bricks around the hole. Be sure to leave a little bit of space between the bricks to allow for ventilation, and to allow rainwater to wash into the hole. The rainwater will help break down solid waste and toilet paper so the hole doesn't fill up so fast.

9. Put the other ten bricks on, making a stack of bricks three layers high. the bricks have notches on the back to make placement easier. The gaps between the bricks will become narrower as you go up.

10. Remember that piece of scrap plywood we told you to get? The one that's two feet by three feet? Take that and cut a hole in it twelve inches in diameter, three inches from one of the long (three foot) sides. You'll need a drill to make a pilot hole and a jig saw to make the round cut. I know you have a drill because everybody does. If you don't have a jig saw, borrow one from a friend or neighbor. Don't buy one. You'll probably never use it again after this, and it's not worth the $29 you'll pay for it.

I happened to have a jig saw that my wife gave me for Christmas four or five years ago. I opened up the box when I put my outhouse together, then put it back in the box and haven't used it since. Now that the round hole is drilled for mine, I don't expect to ever use mine again. Wanna buy it? I'll give it to you for a good price. A hundred bucks…

11. Once the hole is cut, take the toilet seat off of one of your toilets temporarily. Toilet seats come in different sizes, so I can't tell you where to drill the holes. But if you place the toilet seat onto the plywood over the large hole, you can mark it and drill two ¼ holes in the back of the plywood behind the big hole.

This is important because once the apocalypse happens and the water plant goes out, you won't be able to use the toilets in the house anymore. You can therefore remove the toilet seat from the toilet in the house and attach it to the plywood. So make sure you drill those two holes correctly or the seat won't fit to the plywood.

Now that you've marked and drilled the holes, take the seat back into the house and reattach it to the toilet. Nothing pisses a woman off faster than when she sits on a toilet and there's no seat there.

12. Okay, just two more steps and you'll be finished. Next, place the piece of plywood on top of the bricks. Take the four "L" braces and use them to attach the plywood to the fence. Two braces on each side. This is important because it stabilizes the whole thing. Without the braces it'll wobble and may even cause the bricks to collapse.

13. The last step is to take the shower curtain rod out of one of your showers, along with the curtain, and stretch it across the front fence post you just installed and the existing fence. This is your outhouse door, and it's quite effective. And if the wife complains, remind her that she won't be using it in the house anymore anyway.

A couple of notes… Your outhouse is only three feet wide. Some shower curtain rods don't compress that small. If yours doesn't, just take it apart and cut twelve inches off of the male part (reminds me of an old joke, but I won't go there). Use a hacksaw so you don't dent the rod.

Keep a roll of toilet paper in a watertight container. It doesn't have to be fancy. One of those cheap Gladware food containers does quite nicely.

You'll notice that your outhouse doesn't have a roof. Don't freak out. It's designed that way for a couple of reasons.

First of all, it lowers the cost of the project. Secondly, in the early morning, late evening, or on an overcast day, you'll need the light to do your business properly. And last but not least, having no roof allows the occasional rainstorm to wash it for you so it stays spiffy clean.

You can wait until the apocalypse to do this project, but I'd recommend you go ahead and assemble it one Saturday when your favorite sport is out of season and there aren't any games to watch. Here's why:

On the day you need it for real, there will be a lot of crap going on. Having assembled this thing once will make it a lot easier to do it a second time. Also, if you preassemble it now, the holes will already be predrilled and it'll slap together in a fraction of the time.

And here's another tip...

If you don't want the pieces for your outhouse gathering space in the garage while you're waiting for doomsday, you can use them for something else in the meantime. After I assembled mine and then took it apart again, I took the two by fours and fence pickets and made a wall along the west side of my deck, to provide shade from the late afternoon sun. The pieces serve a "peacetime" service, and can be easily called up in time of war.

As for the landscaping bricks? Put them around your trees. That's what they were made for, after all. And your neighbors and friends will never have to know what they'll be used for when the need calls for it.

The hole you dug for the waste should be deep enough to last for at least a couple of years, and probably longer if you get rain on a regular basis. That should be long enough. The world would have to be a pretty ugly place indeed if it took longer than that for your city government to get the water and power systems up and running again.

But just in case your outhouse hole does fill up, it's not that big of a deal. When the waste gets to within a few inches from the top, just unscrew the piece of plywood and set it aside. Then move the bricks out of the outhouse. Dig a new hole a foot in front of the first one, using the first few inches of dirt to top off and cover up the old hole.

Once the new hole is dig, put everything back into place. Your outhouse will be a foot shorter than before, but remember, it was eight feet long to begin with so you still won't be cramped. And now you're good to go for at least two more years.

One last thing. Some of you are asking "why landscaping bricks? Why not just build a wooden box to sit on?"

The short answer is, well, you could just build a wooden box. And you might also save a few bucks.

But… the wooden box would eventually start to sag, and would eventually break. Especially if you have somebody in your group that is a big guy. Like me, for example. I weigh almost 240. It's nearly all muscle, but it's still a lot of weight for a sad piece of plywood to hold up.

The bricks give the seat stability.

And they do something else, too. I'll try not to be too disgusting here…

The bricks give something to direct body waste into the hole beneath the seat. A wayward piece of excrement will bounce off the bricks and go into the hole, instead of landing next to the hole and stinking up the outhouse.

4.
Assessing Your Team's Skills

If you're planning on going it alone when the apocalypse comes, don't freak out. Hear me out. You're going to need at least six responsible people to properly run a security operation.

Some of you may think you can do it by yourself, or with just a couple of others. Say, for example, you, your wife and a couple of small kids.

It may make sense to you. After all, that's fewer mouths to feed, right?

Wrong. Fewer mouths to feed also means fewer people to gather food and water, to defend your home from attack, and to take care of the myriad of other things that'll need to be done.

Again, back to the old adage we talked about before… there is strength in numbers. If you don't have the numbers in your natural group (family or circle of friends), then you'll need to expand your group and bring in some more trusted allies.

It's easy to do. We all have trusted neighbors who've been talking the prepper talk. Or somebody we work with. Or a relative who's close by.

Fill out your team, with people you can trust. And before you go thinking, "Well, there go my food and water stores, with all these mouths to feed," consider this:

Those extra few people you recruit can help you start hoarding stuff. After you assess the person himself to make sure you can trust him, assess two other things as well.

First, assess his skills and what he can bring to the table. If he's good at mechanical things and you're not, that's a plus. When something essential breaks, he's more likely than you are to be able to fix it. If he's a better shot than you are, that's another plus. If he's got weapons and you don't, that's a *very big* plus.

You get the idea. You're not just taking on an extra mouth to feed. You're taking on extra talents and abilities you didn't have before.

The second thing I want you to assess is your prospective team member's financial situation.

It may sound harsh, but some people may not bring much to the table other than an ability to pay for things. And that's okay. Because having money to buy their way into your group is just as good as having other talents.

Say, for example, you work with this guy. His name is Joe. He's a nice enough guy, but kind of a loner. And you know he's got money in the bank because he's always wearing nice clothes, driving a fancy car, and buying the latest video games.

If you can trust him to keep his mouth shut and do what he's told, talk to him about your prepping plans. Tell him you expect a terrorist dirty bomb attack. Or the crash of the American economy. Or a collision with a meteorite. Or whatever you feel in your heart is most likely to happen.

Tell him what the world will be like when that happens. Tell him that chaos will be the order of the day. The commercial districts will be full of looters and rioters. The residential streets will be full of marauders and armed bands of hoodlums, bent on taking what they want from whoever they want.

Tell Joe that he won't able to call the police for help any more. They probably won't be there. They'll probably be at home with their own families, trying to protect their own. And if they are working, they'll have their hands full. If the cops are still on the job, the rioting and lootings and robberies will have them running ragged. Response times will be in the hours, not minutes.

Ask Joe if he'll be able to survive under those conditions.

And when he admits that he can't, offer to let him join your group.

But tell him he has to buy his way in.

Bear in mind that some people are eternal optimists. They see the world through rose colored glasses. You may have to work on Joe a little at a time, over the course of a few weeks or months, to convince him that bad things are coming.

But once you plant that seed in his mind, and fertilize it on a regular basis, he'll eventually come around. Guys like Joe will always come around sooner or later, because they'll realize that all alone they'll be defenseless against the outside world.

Eventually, Joe will accept your offer to join your group.

Then give him a shopping list. Tell him to purchase a gasoline generator capable of carrying a 2000-watt load. And forty sheets of half inch plywood. And forty two by four studs. And two AR-15 rifles with 200 rounds of ammunition. And two 9 mm handguns with 200 rounds of ammunition. And four 4 by 8 sheets of sheet metal. And enough food and water stores to last ten people for a year.

Tell him that's the price of staying alive when the shit hits the fan.

This whole thing with Joe may bother you a bit. Your conscience may try to tell you you're taking advantage of poor Joe.

Tell your conscience to shut the hell up. It doesn't know what it's talking about. Here's why.

Chances are, Joe wouldn't survive on his own in a crisis situation. And if he did somehow manage to do so, he'd spend a hell of a lot more money building his own little mini-fortress than he'll spend on your shopping list.

So you're doing him a favor. You're ensuring his survival. And you're not taking advantage of him. You're merely utilizing the only real tool he has to offer the group: his checkbook.

And speaking of guilt, don't you go feeling guilty either, for bringing on board a guy who is incapable of carrying his own weight.

Even a guy like Joe will be worth his while in your compound. He can pull guard duty, and help entertain the kids. He can process drinking water and tend to the garden and go on supply runs. Bring him aboard, then take him under your wing. Make him a valued member of the team.

5.
Weapons Training

Okay, we touched lightly a minute ago on weaponry. Joe was going to throw two AR-15s and 9 mm handguns into the mix.

You're probably well versed on small arms. Most preppers are. As a general rule, the type of personality that makes a good prepper is the same type that makes him a patriotic American, a lover of God and country, and a man (or woman) who will fiercely protect his family and property at all costs.

So we'll cover just the basics, that a few of you not familiar with small arms may not have thought of.

First of all, I suggested the AR-15 for a couple of reasons. It's a good weapon. It's reliable, doesn't jam as often as an AK-47, is easier to clean and maintain, and stands up better to abuse. Plus, anybody on your team who has been in the military already knows how to use it. Or, at least they know how to use the M-16, which is essentially the same weapon.

I suggested a 9 mm for the same reasons. They are compact, easy to use, and easy to care for. You could use a bigger weapon, sure. But here's the deal. If a 9mm bullet doesn't stop a bad guy before he gets to you, then the chances are a .45 won't either. If you take the proper steps and learn how to shoot, either bullet through the heart or the head will make you the victor every time.

On the other hand, if you already have your own weapons and are comfortable with them, then by all means use them. A couple of things to remember:

You should always share the wealth. And in this case, the "wealth" is knowledge. Every responsible adult in your group, and every child old enough to know when and when not to use a firearm, should be well trained on their use.

Some preppers make a big mistake of designating certain people within their midst as shooters. They're usually chosen for their marksmanship skills, or maybe they're the ones with the most weapons experience and therefore most comfortable with them. And those are all good things.

But what happens in a firefight, if the bad guy gets in a lucky shot and your designated shooter falls over dead with a bullet in his skull?

What will happen in a lot of cases is that the survivors will look at each other and say, "oh, shit."

Because they've never fired the weapon before and don't know how to use it. And then they're screwed, because the bad guys are still shooting and they're not.

What *should* happen is that the dead shooter is dragged to the side and the next person picks up the weapon and takes his place.

That can only happen if the next person, and the one after that and the one after that and the one after that, all know how to handle the weapon and fire it effectively.

Remember, firearms are just tools. And like any other tool, they can make your life a lot easier. But only if they are used properly. If they aren't used properly, they become less of an asset and more of a liability.

Bullets aren't cheap these days, but they're not that expensive, either. Neither is membership at your local gun club. And if the cost is more than you can handle, you don't have to be a member for the rest of your life. Identify your team, join the club, and spend your Saturdays at the range, training your people one at a time on all your weapons. Let them practice until they are proficient shots. Then consider them done and train somebody else.

Of course, if you can handle the cost, maintain your membership so everybody on your team can fire occasionally and stay sharp. But if cost is a factor, get everybody trained, then resign your membership.

Firing a gun is like riding a bicycle. Once you get the fundamentals down, a guy pretty much never forgets them. Unless he's an idiot. And somebody too stupid to fire a gun is somebody you don't want on your team anyway.

If you do resign your membership, you can still have dry fire practices periodically in your back yard. Have everyone on your team go through the motions of loading their mags, sighting in their targets and pulling the trigger. That way they'll stay familiar with the weapon, and it'll be more comfortable for them when it comes time to use it.

It's also important that you teach them proper maintenance. Make sure everybody knows how to take the weapons apart, clean them, and reassemble them.

Okay, here's a tip that you're probably going to laugh at. But it could save your life someday.

Next Fourth of July or New Year's Eve, when all of those fireworks stands are set up just outside your city limits, go visit one of them and get a hundred count pack of Black Cat firecrackers. They make a version with extra powder that makes a bigger bang. Get those.

Take them home and put them in a moisture-proof box, and throw them on a shelf somewhere.

This is just an added insurance policy that will only cost you a couple of bucks, but could be worth a million some day.

You don't know what's going to happen in the months and years ahead. If the situation is so bad that you're holed up in your house for several months or years, and if you've already shot it out with bandits a few times, you may get low on ammo.

That's where the firecrackers come in handy.

They make a good substitute for bullets when you want to scare away prowlers or let somebody know you're armed and mean business.

If you're down to your last few bullets (or even if you're not, but still want to conserve them), all you have to do is light a firecracker inside your house any time you see someone outside who's taking an interest in your house.

The extra loud Black Cat, set off inside your house, will sound like a warning shot to the guy outside. Chances are he'll high-tail it to somebody else's house. Someone who isn't armed and willing to kill him.

And if he doesn't run – if he's too stupid to realize you've just given him a break, then you can still fire a round at his feet to encourage him to run.

Okay, now you've got your weapons and ammo, and you've trained everyone in your group how to use them. Where do you put the weapons?

That's up to you, of course, but I know where I'm putting mine. Each of my sentries, on opposite corners of the house, will have access to one of the AR-15s. They'll be locked and loaded and leaning up in the corner next to the lookout windows. Like any good tool, in its proper place and ready to use.

Of course, your own situation might be a bit different from mine. My children are all teenagers now and grew up knowing how to use and respect firearms.

If your children are younger, or have not been around firearms before, let me give you two suggestions. First, stress to them frequently and in no uncertain terms that they are not to handle the firearms. Never.

Second, because young kids are notorious for doing things they're not supposed to do, take an additional step. Remove the magazines from the AR-15s and put them on safe. Have your sentries carry the magazines.

It only takes an experienced shooter a few seconds to take a magazine from an ammo pouch, load the mag, switch the selector switch to semi, and charge the weapon. Those few seconds are an acceptable trade-off to ensure your youngsters are safe.

As for the handguns, whoever is in charge of the shift will have one. That'll probably be you in the daytime, and your number two man at night. The other one should be carried 24/7 by your best shooter.

Speaking of your best shooter, he should be on your night shift. That's when he's most likely going to be called into action. I'm placing my best shooter on the front window, at night. That'll be the place and time most likely to see action.

I can easily shake him awake if I ever need him in the daytime.

6.
Taking a Human Life

Okay, now we'll take just a minute to discuss the morality of taking another human life. My wife, God bless her, has told me outright that she could never shoot another person.

She was raised in a strict catholic environment and takes every word in the Bible for its literal meaning. She reads the words, "Thou shalt not kill" and sees only black and white. No room for debate. If that's what the Bible says, then so be it.

I point out that the Bible has other passages as well. Like "An eye for an eye, a life for a life." But she doesn't listen. So we've agreed to disagree.

She does accept where I'm coming from, though, even though she doesn't agree with it.

She goes to the range with me. She can break down my weapons as quickly as I can. It takes her longer to reassemble them, but only because she doesn't have the hand or lower arm strength to get the hand guards back into the locking collar.

And she'll never be as good a shot as I am, but she's better than average.

That part doesn't matter anyway, because she assures me she'll never shoot at anything other than targets.

And that doesn't bother me for a couple of reasons. First of all, I respect her position, and it is my intent never to put her in a position to have to shoot anyone. The only way she'll ever be in that position is if I'm dead and there's no one else to protect our children.

Secondly, I know if my heart and soul (and I suspect she does too) that if she ever were the only one left to protect our children, that she would find the strength to take a life. In fact, I'd bet my life on it.

It's incredibly easy for pacifists or people who don't believe in violence to make bold statements. They'll claim that they'll die, or subject themselves to beatings or rape, before they take another life.

But saying and doing are two different things. When faced with certain death, or encountering a band of horny men wanting to bend her or our fifteen year old daughter over the back of a couch, Sarah will do the right thing. She'll fight them off until her last breath. And if there is a weapon within reach, she will fire a bullet through the bastards' heads.

Because our daughter Hannah means more to both of us than life itself. Sarah would break "Thou shalt not kill" and risk going to hell in a heartbeat to save Hannah from being raped or murdered.

I've known this woman for many years. I know what she's capable of even if she doesn't.

My point is this. You may well have members of your group who also profess that they cannot kill another human. And that's fine. My advice is to not argue with them or push the point. Just make sure that they are well trained, and that they know what will likely happen to them if your house is ever overrun and they surrender without a fight.

To the greatest degree possible, protect your fortress. Defend it to your last breath.

Then have faith that when and if the time comes, they'll be able to find the inner strength to blow those assholes away.

Just a side note here… if you don't currently have enough people for your team, and have to recruit more, you'll look closely for what tools they can bring to the table. One thing very high on your wish list is a person with martial arts and self defense skills. Here's why:

When the shit hits the fan, one of the main things you'll have to deal with is boredom. Your group will spend a lot of time holed up in your house, when they're used to getting out and doing things every day. You may or may not have electricity, depending on the type and scope of disaster that has struck your area.

If there is no power, there won't be any TV to watch or computer games to play. Your group will be desperate for things to do.

Someone who knows self defense techniques or martial arts can spend some of that free time working with all the women and kids in your group. That way, if you're dead someday when the bad guys come and can no longer protect them, and if they *don't* have a weapon close by, they'll at least have a fighting chance.

Once the women and girls are well trained, train the boys next. Then, hell, train the men if you want. It'll help everybody pass the time, and could even come in handy for you someday if your weapon jams and you have to do a little hand to hand combat.

7.
Building Your Safe Room

Okay, one last thing about security, and then we'll talk about other stuff for awhile.

Your house needs a safe room. They are ridiculously easy to set up, and aren't as expensive as you might think. Further, they could save your life or the lives of those you love. And that definitely makes it worth your effort.

Remember a couple of chapters back, when we talked about your geeky friend named Joe? The one who had nothing to offer the group other than his checkbook?

Well, hopefully you've found a Joe, or at least know of one. Otherwise you'll be on the hook for forty sheets of plywood, at about sixteen bucks a sheet.

If you can get Joe to cover the cost, have him deliver them to your garage. Lean them up against the walls in the junk side of the garage. You know, that side you call your "work area" that is in reality just a big pile of clutter? Yeah, that space. If you lean them against the wall, they'll be more or less out of the way until the world goes black.

Then they'll be readily accessible when you need them.

Whether you're a handy man or not, your safe room will be the easiest thing you've ever built. I promise.

The concept is simple. When the shit hits the fan, first go into stealth mode by making your house appear vacant (Chapter 1) Then fortify your fence so prowlers will pass by your place and go find a softer target (Chapter 2).

Once that's done, the third thing you should do is build your safe room. If you have at least two men (three would be better), you can build the room within three or four hours.

First, select the room. I'd recommend a large room at the back of the house. In my house, that's the den. When the crisis hits here, my team will carry the plywood from the garage into the den. Then we'll merely stand it up.

When plywood is stood up on its end, it's eight feet high. Coincidentally, so are your living room walls. There should be no trimming or cutting. Just stand up the plywood four sheets thick around the walls, and then nail or screw two by fours into the ceiling (be sure to nail into the studs) to keep them from falling back down.

I sense you have two questions that are just burning a hole in your brain. See if I'm right.

The first question is, "What about the windows?"

The windows are the most vulnerable area in your house, and the most likely entry point if your house ever comes under attack. The more windows you cover the better.

Your second question is, "Is four sheets of plywood enough?"

The answer is yes. That's two inches of pressed wood.

I tested this myself by firing both AR-15 rounds and 9 mm rounds into four sheets of plywood. A couple of the rounds made it to the third sheet, but none made it completely through.

And that's not counting the added protection of your house's outer structure, to include the brick.

Your safe room will provide many things for you.

If, for example, the power grid has been taken out by terrorists, rioters or an EMP, you'll be running off of generator power.

If you've never used generator power before, here's the bad news. They don't have unlimited wattage. I recommend a 2000 watt generator. It's small enough to be reasonably easy on fuel

It's also reasonably quiet, so that you can run it in your garage without the neighbors hearing it.

At the same time, though, a 2000 watt generator is big enough to power your essentials. For example, it'll run a television and a DVD player, a microwave, and a 100 watt light bulb all at the same time. If you put all of those things into your safe room, you can provide a protected, fairly comfortable place for your family or group to hang out and pass their time.

One of the biggest problems you'll have to combat is boredom. Especially if you have kids. Make the safe room the default place for everyone to hang out if they're not on guard duty or doing details. Put board games in there. Books to read. Movies to watch, etc.

In the wintertime, you can run your generator for about two hours a day on a cup of gas. At night during the wintertime, you can run it for another two hours. Only during your nighttime run, you'll operate only two things: a space heater and lights in your safe room. The space heater will draw about 1500 watts. the lights will draw the rest. The space heater will warm the room, and body heat will keep it warm throughout the night.

While your neighbors are buried underneath six blankets on a twenty degree night and still shivering, your group will be fairly comfortable until morning light.

I am lucky in that my part of the country is reasonably mild in the winter time. We don't get a lot of snow and ice, but temperatures do drop into the teens or twenties several nights a year.

As I said, I've already determined that the den on the back of my house will be my safe room. I already have enough plywood and two by fours in my garage to build it. And I've already gone into my attic and doubled the amount of insulation over the den, to help trap winter heat. You should take the same steps.

Besides protecting your group from gunfire, the four sheets of plywood will do an excellent job of masking sound and light. No one will know you have power. But power will make a world of difference in the morale within your group.

8.
Expanding Your Water Storage

I have three kids. Two boys and a girl. All teenagers. They drink an average amount of soda, and my wife has to have her Diet Dr. Pepper. I can take it or leave it, but I'll put away some soda occasionally myself.

We also drink a lot of bottled water. The municipal water supply where I live tastes disgusting. Like horse piss. No, wait. Horse piss probably tastes better, now that I think about it.

The point is this. Everything we drink at my house comes from a bottle.

We used to buy canned sodas, and half liter bottles of water (the ones that come twenty four to a case). Then, a little over a year ago, we stopped. We started buying the two liter bottles of sodas and the one gallon bottles of drinking water.

I *very strongly recommend* you start doing the same, and I can give you several reasons why.

First of all, soda in two liter bottles are ounce for ounce cheaper than sodas in cans. You'll save a few bucks. And every few bucks you save on sodas are a few more bucks you can plug into your food stores or supplies.

Water, also, is cheaper by the gallon than in individual bottles. Again, you can put the money you save aside for your prepping supplies.

You won't notice a big windfall right away, of course. You may not notice it at all. But over the course of a year, you'll save a couple of hundred dollars. For two hundred dollars, you can buy enough spaghetti noodles and chicken bouillon to feed a family of five for three months.

You'll also save money on your electricity bills, while you're waiting for the apocalypse to happen.

Empty water and soda bottles, you see, are light as a feather. And they trap air.

Now, then, pop quiz time: What two properties does insulation have that makes it so effective in keeping your house cool in the summer and warm in the winter?

That's right. Insulation is very light. And it traps air.

In my house, we go through five or six two liter bottles of soda every week. We go through about the same amount of water jugs. And my kids all love milk. We go through three gallons of milk a week also.

We throw them all into a recycling bin in the kitchen. And every few days, when the recycling bin gets full, my wife Sarah gets one of those big black leaf bags, fills it full of empty bottles, and tosses the bag into the garage.

Every few weekends, when I have ten or twelve full bags in the garage and they start getting in the way, I carry them up into my attic.

The first batch I took up there went on top of the den in the back of the house. That's going to be our safe house, remember. Then I started blanketing the entire attic, methodically placing each bag to cover the fiberglas insulation that was already up there.

Now, a little more than a year later, my attic is almost completely covered with a second layer of insulation. It doesn't add any significant additional weight to stress the structure of my house. And I've already noticed a decrease in my electric bills. The house is warmer in the winter than it used to be, and cooler in the summer, and my central heating and air conditioning unit will last longer now because it doesn't have to work as hard as it once did.

But here's the best part of this whole exercise, in case you haven't figured it out yet…

When the power grids go down, and the water plant cannot process or pump drinking water, our neighbors and enemies will be dying of thirst. But not us. We will have a very good supply of drinking water. Because at the first hint of trouble, those hundreds of bottles are coming back down and getting filled with tap water.

In fact, we'll have so much that we'll have the option of bartering some of it for other things we need if we want to.

We'll talk about rain water collection in the next chapter. First, though, a couple of notes about saving empty plastic bottles and storing them in your attic.

The first bag of soda bottles I put in the attic got torn to shreds by a squirrel that somehow got into the attic. After I killed him and plugged the hole he used to get in, I tried to figure out why he'd attack a bag full of empty soda bottles.

It turns out that squirrels like sugar. Some of the bottles in that first bag weren't rinsed well, and the squirrel went after the sugary residue in the bottom of the bottle.

Here's the second thing to remember: always put the caps back on the bottles. The bottles cannot trap air and help insulate your house if the lid is not on. And even more importantly, when you use these bottles for rainwater collection, you'll have to have the caps to seal them.

The third thing is optional. It's something Sarah and I do, just to make our water collection more efficient when the time comes.

Before each empty bottle goes into the leaf bag, we remove the label. Then we take a permanent black marker and write a big "R" on the bottle. This isn't mandatory, but we think it's a good idea. And here's why:

When the rains come, everyone in the group, except the two sentries, will be scrambling. The idea is to collect as much of the rain water as humanly possible. We have at least a thousand empty bottles up in our attic, and our goal will be to fill every last one of them if we can.

Once they're filled, we'll need a way to differentiate between the unpurified rain water, which won't be safe to drink, and the drinking water which has been purified and is therefore safe.

We'll hold back a few bottles that won't have an "R" on them. Once the water is processed, we'll place the safe water in the unmarked bottles. The big "R" on the rain bottles will act as a big red flag to everyone in our group to not drink it.

9.
Why Rainwater is Important

Let's face it. We've all become dependent on the water always being available from the faucet whenever we need it. It's handy, the water is safe, and it'll always be there for us.

But what if it isn't?

In an emergency, whatever its nature, there's a good chance the city water supply will be disrupted. Or contaminated. The vast majority of Americans won't know what to do or where to go. They won't be prepared.

But you will. Here's how.

First of all, buy yourself ten cases of drinking water for each person in your household. You don't have to do it all at once. In fact, it's better to buy a couple of cases at a time. Say, each time you make a grocery run. If any of your neighbors saw you unloading forty cases of water and putting them in your garage, guess where they're coming when the stuff hits the fan? That's right. Your place. And they may not ask politely.

The bottled water is only a temporary measure, of course. It's not intended to last you forever, only until the next rain. And if you took my earlier advice and stored empty bottles in your attic, and were able to fill them while the water was still pumping, you won't need the cases of drinking water.

Unless you live in the desert, your area will provide you enough rainfall to stay alive long after

the bottled water runs out. You have to be prepared
to have a place to store it once you catch it, though.

****

NOTE: If you live in God-forsaken Nevada, or
anywhere else in the desert southwest, you'll have
to modify these plans. That's because in certain
areas of the United States, there simply isn't enough
rainfall to keep your needs met.

Notice I didn't say to abandon these plans. Even
Las Vegas or Phoenix gets an occasional downpour,
and if you're not ready for it, all that precious water
will slip through your fingers.

If you live in a very dry area, the procedures
we're getting ready to discuss still apply to you, and
you still need to do them. But you also need to take
extra steps because of the lack of rainfall in your
area. A few paragraphs back, I said to stockpile ten
cases of water for every person in your group. For
you people who live in the desert, make that twenty
cases per person. I know. That's a lot of water. If
your garage won't hold it, line a couple of the
bedroom walls with it. Downstairs bedrooms. Not
the upstairs, because weight will be a problem.

If you have children, you've probably already
noticed they don't give a damn what their rooms
look like.

In my son Jordan's room, one outer wall is
covered, from wall to wall, with cases of Sam's
Club water, stacked four cases high. I cut plywood
the same width and ran it along the top of the water.
Now it's a convenient shelf for his sports trophies
and photos of his girlfriends. He doesn't care. He's

a teenaged boy, for crying out loud. And we all know that teenaged boys are barely human, am I right?

Also, if you live in a desert climate, familiarize yourself with the playa lakes in your area. The idea is to be ready for the occasional rainfall so you can capture as much as possible. If you're well prepared and saved your empty soda and water bottles, you might get lucky and catch all you need.

If you run out, use the cases of drinking water as your backup. But use it for drinking only. No laundry, no bathing. The females in your family won't like that, but it's a necessary evil. Tell them to pretend they're camping and suck it up.

Make nightly excursions to a local pond or river, or whatever other water source is close by. Take pieces of rope or bungee cords about two feet long. Tie each end to the handle of a gallon sized water bottle. You can drape the ropes over your shoulders and carry four gallons of water and still keep your hands free for carrying a weapon, if you think you'll need one.

If you don't think you'll need a weapon, you can use your hands to carry an additional two gallons.

Bear in mind, though, that six gallons of water weigh almost fifty pounds. That's a lot of weight for anyone to carry any considerable distance. Don't attempt it unless you're in very good shape.

Shortly, we'll cover procedures to sanitize water and make it safe to drink. If you're processing pond water, pay extra close attention, and follow the instructions to the letter. People with strong dispositions might be able to cut some corners and drink rain water without any significant problems.

Pond water is a different story. If you drink pond water that hasn't been properly processed, you're begging for problems.

****

Okay, to summarize…

Anyway, regardless of where you live, you'll need to be adequately prepared when the rain comes. Start now. If your family drinks soda, as most families do, stop buying the cans. Start buying the two liter bottles. It's cheaper anyway.

And stop throwing the bottles away. When they're empty, rinse them out well, then place the caps back on them. Then put them aside.

Do the same for plastic milk containers and gallon water bottles.

When you have enough to fill up a plastic trash bag, fill it up with the empty bottles and take it up to the crawlspace in your attic.

Place it in the corner of your crawlspace, on top of the existing insulation. It'll be light so it won't cause any stress on the ceiling. And by capping the bottles, they will trap air, and therefore make excellent secondary insulation.

Over the course of a few months or a year, depending on how much milk and water your family drinks, you might be able to cover every square inch of attic or crawlspace. Your heating and cooling bills will go down. But here's the best part about this tip…

If the water supply is ever disrupted, you'll be forced to survive on rain water. And those who aren't prepared will watch precious rain slip right through their fingers and onto the ground. Simply because they don't know how to catch it or have nothing to store it in.

If you have a couple of hundred empty plastic bottles you can drag out of your attic for a rainstorm, you'll be able to store all you need until the next rainstorm. And you may even be able to store enough to barter with your neighbors for other things you need. Like food or fuel.

Cost of this: Nothing. You're using containers that you normally throw out anyway. And by doing this, you're saving money on heating and cooling costs until the apocalypse, and ensuring yourself an adequate supply of water afterwards.

In the next three chapters, we'll talk about three easy and low cost methods of collecting rain water in a suburban setting. All three can be done on the cheap, and on the down-low. If you do it right, there is absolutely no reason your neighbors will ever know. And therefore no reason for them to see your house as a target when they run low.

Of course, if you like your neighbors, you can share these methods with them. But if you're going to do that, do it before the apocalypse instead of after, since they will require a little bit of preparation on your neighbor's part.

As for that neighbor who always walks his dog past your house and lets the dog crap in your yard? Screw him. Let him fend for himself.

10.
Collecting Rain Water, Method 1

Okay, now that you have the means to store a large amount of water, there are several means of collecting it. A smart prepper will utilize all of them.

The smartest and easiest method of collecting rainwater is through a series of rain gutters, attached to your house. Most people don't have them on the back side of their house, but that's exactly where you want yours.

Here's why: When the stuff hits the fan, you don't want any of your neighbors to see you collecting rain water. Especially if you have the means to collect and store a large amount of it. Because if they see you catching and storing two hundred gallons of rain water, and they could only store a few gallons because they didn't plan ahead and have nothing to store it in, then they're coming to see you when they run out.

You may not have a problem sharing a little water with your friends. Except that the word will get out. And the scarcer water is, the faster word will travel. And if people with no water are desperate, they won't hesitate to take it by force.

Okay. The good news is that rain gutter is relatively cheap and is easy to install. Install it all the way across the back of your house. Put a downspout on each corner.

Good. Now you're almost done, but not quite. Now get several large garbage cans. Not the kitchen kind. Get those great big green suckers that you use to put your garbage in on trash pickup day. Be sure to get the ones with the snap-on lids.

Only don't use them for trash. Put them in your garage and leave them there.

If the stuff ever hits the fan and the water supply is disrupted, take them and put them in your back yard. One next to each of the downspouts. The downspouts will come in sections. Take the last sections off, and the bottom of the spouts will be a few feet above the ground. Place one of the trash cans under each spout. Be sure to keep the lids on the cans after the rain stops so your rainwater won't evaporate on sunny days.

At the first hint of rain, remove the lids and let the water fall from the roof and into the trash cans.

But wait, you're not finished yet.

You don't want the trash cans to overflow and waste precious water.

Remember all those empty soda and milk bottles up in your attic? Drag them down. Dip them into the trash cans full of rainwater and fill them up. But only fill them three quarters of the way full. More on that later.

If you haven't already done it, write a big "R" on each of the bottles you fill. That way everyone in your group will know that it is unprocessed rain water and is not safe to drink.

Obviously, this requires a little bit of preparation on your part ahead of time. You can either buy the gutter and trash cans when your budget allows it and keep them in your garage until they're needed, or you can buy them and install them ahead of time. That way they're out of your way and it's one less thing to worry about when you need them. Also, when the apocalypse happens, you may not have electricity. Rain gutter is a hell of a lot easier to install with power tools. It can be done without power tools, but it'll take a lot longer and your small children standing below you watching will learn some colorful new words.

We'll discuss in a bit how to purify the rainwater so it's safe to drink. In the meantime, remember this… Don't stop storing water until the rain stops, or until you fill up every container you own. You can never, ever have too much water. If you have more than what you need, no problem. Somebody out there will be desperate to get it, and will be willing to trade you anything they have to get it.

It's always better to be the one looking out instead of the one looking in. You want to be the guy who has the water. Not the guy who's desperate to get it.

The cost of this method of collecting rainwater varies, of course, based on where you live, where you buy your hardware, and how long your roofline is. I guttered the back of my house and bought four trash cans with lids for less than $300. And it doesn't have to be done all at once. You can buy a little at a time if you need to.

11.
Collecting Rainwater, Method 2

Like we said earlier, you don't have to be rich or invest your life's savings to be an effective prepper. A lot of the best methods don't cost much at all.

We also said that there are three very effective ways to catch rainwater. Smart preppers use all three. You never know when the next rainfall is coming; therefore you can never have too much water.

The second method requires two fence posts, a twelve by twenty foot plastic tarp with grommets, and a box of nails. Total cost: About fifty bucks. If you can't put rain gutters on your house for whatever reason, use this method. It's the cheapest and easiest of the three.

Oh, you'll need a set of post hole diggers again. If you don't have a set, borrow your neighbor's for a couple of hours. If you can afford a pair of your own, though, go ahead and buy some. Keep them in your garage. they'll come in handy for other things as well.

We're assuming your back yard had one of those six foot high privacy fences. Unless you live in the country or an apartment building, you probably do. If you have another kind of fence in your back yard, you can still use this method. Just modify it slightly to fit your needs.

Anyway, most privacy fences have three pieces of two by fours that run between the posts and have slats nailed to them. The top two by four should be about head high or a little lower.

Lay out your 12 by 20 tarp. See those holes along the edges with little brass rings embedded to keep the tarp from tearing? Those things are called grommets. A 12 by 20 tarp will have five grommets on the long side and three on the short side.

Hammer five nails into the top two by four. Don't nail them in all the way. They need to line up with the grommets, so that you can place the grommets over the nails. Hang one side of the tarp onto the fence.

Now, twelve feet away from your fence, use your post hole diggers to plant your fence posts. You don't need cement. In fact, it's better if you don't use any. Just be careful when you dig the hole so it's not too wide. You'll only need the holes occasionally, when it rains, so when the weather is dry you can pull the posts back up and put them out of the way.

Here's the important part. Your tarp is twenty feet wide. Your fence posts need to be a bit less than that. Say, eighteen feet wide. That will create a low spot on the open side of the tarp so the water will be able to run off into your rain barrel, or bucket, or whatever you're going to use to catch the water.

Be sure to dig the holes deep enough so that the tarp is a bit lower on the open end than on the fence end. Also, hammer a nail halfway into the top of each of the fence posts so you can hook the tarp to them.

During a moderate to heavy rain storm, a 12 by 20 tarp will catch a lot of water. Be sure you're standing by with empty water jugs or soda bottles to catch it all and store it. Any water you don't catch is gone forever.

I'll be using large 50 gallon garbage cans to capture my water, but there's an alternate method. If you've been in Walmart, or any other department store, you've seen those plastic storage tubs they sell. They cost six or eight bucks apiece and come with plastic lids that usually snap into place.

If you don't want to use the trash cans, buy some of these tubs. Use them to place under the center of the tarp on the open end. That will be the lowest part of the tarp, and since the fence posts aren't quite as wide as our tarp, the weight of the rain water will form a "V" in the tarp that will channel every drop of water into the tub.

Then it's just a matter of having someone drag all those empty bottles down from the attic and bring them to you. You'll submerge each bottle into the water, cap it, and give it to someone to carry into the house.

Put a responsible adult on each tub and rain barrel. They have to be quick, though. During a heavy rainfall, the tubs will fill quickly. Do not let them overflow. The water is too precious to lose.

12.
Collecting Rain Water, Method 3

If you have a garage or low roof on your structure, or if you live on a zero lot line property and have a neighbor's house that overlooks your yard, this method is ideal for you.

What you'll essentially be doing here is making a makeshift rain gutter system.

Here's the short list of what you'll need: six two by four studs, eight feet long; eighteen two inch "L" braces, a hand powered drill, a small tube of caulking and some one inch long screws. Total cost: $80.

The "L" braces are L shaped pieces of steel, two inches long on each side, with two holes in each side. They can be found in any hardware shore or on Walmart's hardware aisle.

Keep these items in your garage. Save them until doomsday arrives and the water source is disrupted. I don't want you to do this method until the shit actually hits the fan, because if you don't do it properly, you could cause the roof to leak.

Now, that wouldn't bother you much once doomsday hits. But if you did this now to get a jump on things, and if doomsday didn't happen for five more years, and your roof started to leak, you'd blame me. So just keep the stuff in the garage until you need it.

Building your makeshift gutter is a piece of cake. All you do is climb up on a low hanging rooftop, lay out the two by fours in a "V" shape, leave a one foot gap in the center for the water to drain through, and fasten the two by fours to the roof with the "L" braces and screws.

It makes sense to pre-drill your holes in the two by fours ahead of time. We wouldn't recommend installing the "L" braces until you need them, though. The lumber will stack in your garage much easier if you don't. Be sure you mark the two by fours with the holes drilled in them so that you can find them easily later, and so that you don't use them for something else.

We're assuming that if something happens that's bad enough to kill your water supply, then your power grid is probably out too. Even if you pre-drill the holes in your lumber, you won't be able to pre-drill the holes in the roof. A hand-powered drill would come in very handy. You should have one of those anyway. Later in the book we'll tell you how to do a lot of other things. And we'll assume you'll have no electrical power. So a twelve dollar investment in a hand drill will come in handy.

If you live on a zero lot line property and your neighbor's roof drains into your yard, and if you're planning on using his roof to collect the water, make some kind of deal with him ahead of time. Say for example, give him half the water that comes from his roof. It's only fair, after all, and you're still coming out ahead. Because you're getting the other half.

A couple of things about building your makeshift rain gutter: When you install the two by fours onto the roof, put the narrow side of the wood against the roof. You'll catch three times as much rain that way. You're probably thinking, "Well, duh, that's a no brainer." But we're working under the assumption that you have no carpentry skills whatsoever and need to be told these things.

In case you haven't already figured it out, the caulking is to squirt into each hole you drill into the roof, before you insert the screw. That should stop any leaks, at least for the near term. Over a period of several months, leaks will develop, but they'll be small ones. And in a survivalist type environment, that'll be the least of your worries.

One last thing about this one, and then I'll shut up. You'll install the two by fours in the shape of a "V" with a one foot gap in the middle. You'll have three pieces of wood on each side. Be sure you overlap each successive piece of wood about a foot over the one beneath it, so you don't lose any water under the seams. And don't forget to put a rain barrel or large tub underneath the bottom of the "V" to catch the runoff.

This method won't catch all of the water. The two by fours won't be flush against the asphalt shingles, and some water will escape beneath them. But during a heavy rainstorm, this method can capture ten to twenty gallons of water per minute, and it can be a very effective way of enhancing your water supply.

13.
Collecting Water During The Winter

Yes, you can, and you should. Granted, it's cold outside and you don't want your little tootsies to freeze. But suck it up, buttercup. I can't say this enough. *Never* pass up an opportunity to collect water. Even when it's in the dead of winter and twenty degrees outside.

I can see you rolling your eyes and hear you ask, "How can you collect rain when it's frozen?"

Easy. You've heard of a snow shovel, right?

Just so we understand each other, I'm not talking about shoveling the snow off your driveway and sidewalks. It may be tempting, but don't forget you're in stealth mode. Nobody clears the sidewalks of a vacant house, so that would be a dead giveaway.

However... snow shovels work even on grass, and as long as you have a place to put it, you should collect as much snow from your back yard as you possibly can.

Put in the rain barrels you have in the back yard. When they get full, dump them into a bathtub, then go out for more.

I know. There's dirt and leaves and maybe even dead bugs in the ice and snow from your back yard. Why collect dirty ice and snow that you're never gonna want to use?

I'll give you two good reasons.

First, If you saved the empty bottles like I recommended, and get even an average amount of rainfall in your area, then chances are you'll never have to drink this particular water.

But your crops will love it in the spring and summer. They're nowhere near as picky or squeamish as you are. And the more melted ice and snow you have in your barrels, the less better, cleaner water you'll have to give them if you have a long period of time between rainfalls.

The second reason is that you claim you'll never drink backyard water. But the truth is, you will in a pinch. If that's the only water left to drink, you'll strain it and purify it (we'll tell you how later) and you'll be happy to have it. Seriously.

14.
Storing Your Rainwater

Okay, I'll say this again in case you haven't gotten the hint yet. You can never have enough water. It can be used to drink and barter for other things you need. During the growing season you'll need it to grow stuff.

One thing you never, ever want to do is pass up the chance to gather as much as you can. That's why I provided you with three means for catching rainwater and suggested you use all three.

Don't ever, *ever* say "that's enough" during a rainstorm. The only good excuse for stopping your collection efforts is when you run out of things to put water in.

And if you've taken our advice and saved your empty milk and water jugs, and your empty soda bottles, you should have the capability to store hundreds of gallons.

I had a guy on my team (until recently) who said we only needed to have a hundred bottles of water.

He said, "If we have any more water than that, we won't have a place to store it all."

As I said, he's no longer on my team. I have no room for idiots.

Having too much water is like having too much money.

At least I think it is. I've never had too much money. But I think if I did, I'd find some way to spend it.

Water is the same way. We'll catch as much water as we can, or until we run out of containers to put it in. Finding a place to put it is a problem I'll happily deal with.

I think I've mentioned before that you shouldn't fill the bottles all the way full. You don't want them to freeze and shatter. You'll lose not only the water, but the bottle as well.

When it rains, take those plastic bottles and fill them three quarters of the way full. Store them in your house standing up. Don't lay them down and try to stack them. The bottles on the bottom won't hold up to the weight and the caps will start to drip after awhile. Even if you have several hundred such bottles, they won't take up a lot of space. All you have to do is line your base boards with them. Put them under the beds. Fill your cupboards with them. Cover the floor in your garage. If you no longer have electrical power, fill your refrigerator with them. It's not doing any good for you anyway.

The point is, even if you have several hundred bottles of water, keep collecting it. There's never enough. Really.

If you haven't already done it, take a sharpie or other type of permanent water and write a very large "R" on every bottle you have, except for a couple of dozen or so. Leave those blank.

That's how you'll tell which is unpurified rainwater, and which water is safe to drink.

Here's how it works, in a nutshell. You gather the water in the bottles marked with an "R." And every few days, when your fresh water bottles start to get empty, you purify a new batch of rainwater until it's safe to drink. Then you pour the safe water into the unmarked bottles. Simple concept, huh?

Yeah, I thought so too…

A couple more notes. Resist the urge to purify the water until you start to run low. That's because it'll take a lot of your fuel to purify the water. You don't want to spend a lot of fuel to purify it all, and then run out of unpurified water for your crops. If that happens, you'll have to use your drinking water to water your crops, and the fuel you used to purify it will have gone to waste.

But even this rule has an exception. Going into the winter months, you need to purify enough water to get you through the winter. Here's why.

When the temperature is moderate or warm, it takes a lot less fuel to boil a pot of water.

In the winter, you burn three to four times as much fuel to boil the same pot of water. That's because the fire is competing against the air temperature. The fire is trying to heat the water, and the air temperature is trying to keep the water cold. It's much better to prep your winter water before the winter actually gets there. Fill up all the unmarked bottles you have, then take advantage of every day when the temperatures are moderate to repeat the process.

15.
Purifying Water

Okay, we've talked a lot about collecting rainwater. Now let's talk about how to purify it.

Theoretically, rainwater should be safe to drink, since it is just water that evaporates and then condensates. And that would be true, if you could indeed catch rainwater in its pure form.

The problem is that as water falls through the air it collects all kinds of particles. Dust, pollens, ash and pollutants. So by the time it goes splat on your roof, it's already been tainted.

Then, as it rolls off the roof and into your rain gutter, and then into your rain barrel, it collects other stuff as well. Like the bird shit that's on your roof. Or the dirt blown onto the shingles from that dust storm last month.

And let's not forget that the shingles are made of asphalt. And asphalt, like any other petroleum based product, gives off a certain amount of chemical residue.

Not enough to kill you outright, of course. But if you drank rain water coming off an asphalt room for years, it could start causing serious health problems. Like cancer of the stomach or liver, for example.

The rain water you collect on the plastic tarp attached to your fence will be a bit cleaner. It'll still have all the nasty stuff from the atmosphere it collects while falling down to earth, of course. But it won't have any of the chemicals from the roof shingles.

And, assuming that you keep the tarp rolled up when it's not raining, it won't have any of the bird shit in it either.

Whichever method you use to catch your rainwater, though... whether it comes from the tarp method or off the roof, it all needs to be processed before it's safe to drink. Untreated rainwater should only be consumed under emergency conditions. Some people with strong digestion systems might be able to drink it and get away with it. But for most people, it can lead to serious stomach issues, such as vomiting, dry heaves, diarrhea and dehydration. So you're best off not trying to drink it unless you have to.

The preferred method to sanitize rainwater is simply to boil it for ten minutes. It's also the easiest method.

Of course, any method of boiling would work. You could build a campfire, or even put a pot of water on a barbeque grill. That's up to you.

I'll tell you what I've got planned. You can adopt my method, or select another.

I bought a Coleman camp stove at Walmart. It's a portable burner that screws onto the top of a small bottle of propane. I think the stove cost me about $48 or so. Not bad.

The bottles of propane come two to a pack at Walmart, for $4.88. Each bottle burns for about eight hours, or sixteen hours of burn time total, for less than five bucks.

I actually did a test to see how much water I could boil for ten minutes on a bottle of propane. On a nice day last spring, my daughter Hannah and I spent a day pouring, bottling and measuring. On a single bottle of propane, we were able to treat a little over a hundred gallons of water.

Remember that the bottles come in a two-pack. That's two hundred gallons of drinking water for five bucks. Not bad.

Every time I go to Walmart I go back to the camping section and throw a two-pack of propane into my cart. I haven't counted lately, but I believe I have sixty to seventy bottles now. I could probably cut it off, but it's become a habit. A habit I'll probably continue to do until all hell breaks loose.

Then I'll be glad to have it.

As I said, your choice of building a fire and purifying water is up to you. I chose a method that is both convenient and economical. The fire burns at a consistent rate, unlike charcoal or wood fires. I personally think it's the way to go.

Okay, once you decide your burn method, build a fire. Take a large stew pot and fill it with rainwater.

But don't just dump the rainwater in. You have to filter it first, to catch any solid impurities, like pieces of leaves or tiny pieces of shingles. Or lumps of bird shit that haven't dissolved.

The best way to do this is to take three or four clean cotton socks. Used socks will work, but I'd recommend new ones bought specifically for this purpose.

Put the socks within each other, and then wrap them over the neck of the bottle of rainwater. Pour the rainwater through the socks and into the stew pot.

Watch the water. It must boil for at least ten minutes to kill all the microorganisms and germs. It doesn't hurt it to boil it longer than that. However, the longer it boils the more you'll lose to evaporation. So I'd shoot for as close to ten minutes as possible.

Once it's finished boiling, take it off the fire and set it aside to cool. Then put another pot on and repeat the process.

Make a note of this, it's very important. You want to keep your rainwater water bottles and your drinking water bottles completely separate. If you pour the clean water back into a bottle marked "R", you've tainted it again and will have to redo it. Only put it into unmarked bottles.

And make sure that everyone in your group knows not to drink from the marked bottles. They'll probably pay a heavy price if they do.

Also important: Let the water cool completely before you pour it into the unmarked bottles. Like the roofing shingles, plastic bottles are also a petroleum based product. And like all petroleum based products, they tend to leach chemicals. Normally it's too slight to be of any concern. However, pouring hot water into a plastic bottle will cause the chemicals to leach much more easily into your drinking water. Once it's completely cool, it's okay to do the transfer.

16.
Other Purification Methods

Okay, we've talked about boiling your rainwater. That *should* be your go-to method for purifying your water. But there are other methods you can use as well.

If you are out of fuel, or trying to conserve it, you can also kill bacteria with chlorine bleach. it's not quite as safe, but it's your second best option.

You need to pour the rainwater through your sock filter from one rainwater bottle into another empty rain water bottle. This may sound strange, but there's a purpose for it.

The chlorine you use to treat the water with will easily kill the bacteria in the water itself. But anything solid, any particulate, that is contaminated, is tougher for the chlorine to clean. And if it remains in the water, it can recontaminate the water after the chlorine has done its job.

So transfer the rainwater from one marked bottle, through the socks, and into a similar bottle.

Take an eye dropper. You may not think you have one around the house, but I'll bet if you looked, you'd find one. If you can't find one, take a bottle of Visine. Empty it out. Purge it by squeezing it and dipping it into a bowl of hot water. Then release it while underwater, so that it fills itself with hot water. Do this several times to get all the Visine out. Then fill it with bleach the same way.

If it's warm and sunny outside, put five drops of bleach into a two liter bottle. Eight drops for a three liter bottle. Then place the bottle outside, in direct sunlight, until it's warm to the touch for at least an hour.

After that, the water is safe to drink.

If it's cold outside, or overcast, you'll have to increase the chlorine. try eight drops for a two liter bottle and thirteen drops for a three liter bottle. Set it aside for several hours.

Okay, this method has several notes that go along with it.

First of all, you must use clear bottles so that the sun can help purify the water. Colored bottles will keep the water cool and hinder the sun's ability to help you. 7-Up bottles are out for this method.

Also, the bottle needs to be shaken several times during the process. This will help agitate the water and mix the chlorine more thoroughly. It will also wash down any contaminants from the neck of the bottle, above the water line.

Third, you'll be tempted to overdo the bleach. Don't. A little bit of bleach goes a very long way. Seriously. If you overdo the bleach, the water will taste nasty. Then (especially if it's hot) your people might start getting dehydrated simply because they avoid drinking the water.

Once the water is safe to drink, don't forget to transfer it to an unmarked bottle. You don't want your team to get into the habit of drinking from marked bottles, even if they think it's safe to do so. If you let that happen, you're asking for trouble. Eventually, someone will drink from a marked bottle, thinking it's been sanitized. And it won't be.

Like I said, a little bleach goes a long way.

In our house, we keep a large bottle of Clorox in the laundry room, and two in the garage. Every once in awhile my lovely wife Sarah, who is beautiful but slightly scatterbrained, will run out of bleach while she's doing laundry. She'll sneak into the garage and pilfer one of our prep bottles, but she always replaces it next time she goes shopping.

One last thing. I don't have a swimming pool, but I have a ten pound case of HTH in my garage. HTH is powdered chlorine. It's used to clean swimming pools. Walmart sells it on their swimming pool aisle, although it's hard to find during the winter months.

I have it because it doesn't take up much space, and because it does the same thing liquid bleach does. Instead of using a dropper, just put a small pinch of powder into the bottle, shake well, and process as described above.

17.
Pond Water

For those of you who live in desert regions who may resort to drinking pond water occasionally, I have good news and bad news for you.

The good news is, there is a method for making pond water safe to drink.

The bad news is that it takes a lot longer, and the water tastes... well, pretty nasty when you're done.

But it's doable. To process pond water, drain it thoroughly through the cotton socks to catch all solid materials. The socks will also capture most of the green pond scum.

Boil the water for at least twelve minutes, with half a teaspoon per gallon of table salt. This will give it a very slight salty taste, but it will help break down the microorganisms in the water so that the boiling can kill them easier.

After the water cools, pour it into an unmarked (drinking water) bottle. But wait, you're not finished yet. It still needs five drops of chlorine bleach and to sit in the sun for a day (or eight drops of chlorine if there is no sun) to finish the process.

I have to tell you, I've purified pond water several times, and despite all the work you put into it, it still tastes bad. Kind of a cross between fishy and dirty.

But here's a solution...

Stockpile some powdered drink mix. Walmart sells little canisters of it. Each canister comes with six packets of flavoring. Each packet will flavor a two liter bottle of pond water. Cost of each canister is $1.78. Not much, considering…

Okay, two more things, and then we'll get off the whole water thing and talk about something else.

As I've said before, water is better than gold in a survival situation. You cannot possibly have too much of it. Grab every opportunity that comes along to grab it. If it's raining and all of your bottles are filled, pour some bottles into your bathtubs and then fill them back up with rainwater.

Yes, it's that important.

Keep an eye on the changing seasons. You know better than I how soon the weather starts getting cold in your area, and how low the temperatures can drop.

If you live in Arizona, this part doesn't apply to you. But if you live in a northern state, you may want to pay attention.

A couple of weeks before you expect your first freeze, take a look at all your stored water. You need the top third of the bottles to be air going into a hard freeze. Anything less than that and there's a possibility that the bottle will burst. Not only will you lose the water, you'll lose the bottle as well. Your ability to catch and store more water in the future is diminished a little with every bottle you lose.

If you have several hundred bottles, like we expect to, this can be a very big deal. Taking our full bottles and lessening each one by a third will be time consuming and a pain in the ass. But it must be done.

You can obviously start by utilizing all the empty bottles you have. Once you fill them up, fill your bathtubs. You don't use the tubs anymore anyway, so what does it matter, right?

After the tubs, fill every pot and pan in the house, except for the ones you cook with and boil water in. Then fill your rain barrels outside. Don't forget to put the lids on them to prevent evaporation.

Once all of those have been exhausted, get creative. Blow up that kiddie pool in the back closet and put it into the garage. Make a water bed out of that air mattress.

The point is, do whatever it takes to avoid sacrificing any water. If it looks like a hard freeze is on the way, and if you have no more vessels to put the extra water in, then use it to water your fruit trees. At least it'll do a little bit of good.

Last thing about water (YAY!)... I almost hate to mention this, because it's really a no brainer.

The trouble with no brainers is that really smart people get so caught up in current situations that they sometimes do incredibly dumb things.

Or forget all about the most basic things that need to be done.

So here's the deal. If the earth, as I believe, will be bombarded with EMPs in the next few years, it will happen with little or no warning. Sometimes scientists warn us a day in advance of solar storm activity, sometimes they don't.

So if that's what causes the apocalypse, there will be little to no chance of making advance preparations.

However, many other crises (yes, that's a word, I looked it up) will provide us with a little bit of warning.

Say, for example, you see a story on the news that a terrorist group is claiming they have dirty bombs and are getting ready to attack us with them. Or, an airplane is hijacked somewhere in your region and they've gone silent. Or, the Air Force does an inventory and determines that some of its air launched nuclear weapons are somehow missing.

Or any one of a hundred other things you see or hear about that make you go, "oh shit…"

Those things should be your go signal. That's when you spring into action. You don't actually wait until the power goes out and the faucets go dry. You start pulling those bottles down from the attic and filling up as many as possible.

And if you watch the news the next day, and the Air Force made an honest mistake? If they determined the terrorist threat was just a hoax? If the airplane wasn't hijacked after all, they just lost their radio contact?

No big deal. So it was a false alarm. You didn't lose anything. You didn't waste a single drop of water. You can still use it to fill your sink when you wash dishes, or to pour into your toilet when the toilet needs to be flushed, or to water the daisies in the front yard. You can still make use of it.

But, you got some practice. And that's a good thing. And you know what to do the next time something like that happens.

That's a much better thing.

18.
Laundry? Seriously?

Sarah drives me crazy sometimes, but she's a great wife and a much better person than I'll ever be. So every once in awhile I will give into her.

She asked me to devise a way she could do laundry after the apocalypse comes. Just so that occasionally the pigs in the family (she was referring to me and our boys) didn't smell like, well… pigs.

I've told her that if the power grid ever does go down, and takes the city water plant with it, it will likely be only temporary. Only a few months or a couple of years at the outside.

"And besides," I said, "Guys don't mind smelling like pigs sometimes. It's just one of those things that makes it so much fun to be guys."

"I know it will be temporary," she said. "But it would be nice if occasionally, even after none of us have bathed in a year, if we could put on something clean and just smell nice for a change."

I'm not a henpecked husband by any stretch of the imagination. Nor am I "whipped." If you women aren't familiar with the term "whipped," ask your husband to explain it to you. I'm not going to.

Anyway, my point is that I don't roll over every time my lovely wife demands something. But I'll be the first one to admit that she's put up with an awful lot of crap from me over the years. So it's only fair that occasionally I offer her a little concession.

So, when the apocalypse hits and the power grid goes down, the city water plant will not be able to process water or pump it into our home. We'll rely on stored water and bottled water to survive.

And yes, we put our heads together and devised a way to do laundry.

Remember those storage tubs we talked about earlier? The ones from Walmart?

Well, by our back door sit two of those tubs, stacked one inside the other. When the apocalypse happens, that's where we'll start throwing our dirty shirts and underwear.

And when rainstorms happen after that, the rest of our group (minus the two sentries) will be out in the back yard gathering rainwater.

Except for my dear wife Sarah.

Sarah will be in the rain with us. But she will be feverishly scrubbing the laundry in those two buckets, using rainwater and a handful of Tide detergent. And when she gets done, she will hang each piece of laundry on a long piece of heavy wire I've already strung along the side fence, from the back porch to the far corner of the yard. The rain will rinse the soap out (hopefully) and the sun will dry the laundry when it comes out after the rainstorm.

She paced it off and figured she can wash and hang forty to fifty pieces of laundry each time it rains. Will that be enough to do all of our laundry and keep us all smelling like roses?

Probably not. But it'll help. And more importantly, it made my wife happy.

And we all know that's ultimately the most important thing in the world. Right, guys?

By the way, Sara did make one concession of her own. If it rains so much that every other container we own is full, and we need her to laundry buckets to save more water, she'll give them up. She'll probably be done by then anyway.

Likewise, if we sense a freeze coming and we're scrambling to downsize our stored water bottles, and we need a place to pour some of the water, she'll give them up then too.

She actually didn't mind agreeing to that. She said there's no way she would ever go into a freezing rain to do laundry. Apparently it's okay for us to smell like pigs under those circumstances.

19.
Strength in Numbers

Okay, we've made you invisible to your neighbors and we've fortified your property, all at very little cost.

The next step in your security costs you absolutely nothing, but it could save your life.

Actually, depending on the size and ages of your family members, and your circle of friends, you may already have this one covered. If not, I'm going to explain why it's so important and very strongly suggest that you pay particularly close attention to it.

There is strength in numbers. That's always been the case, in pretty much any battle situation. If armies are more or less equal as far as the types of weaponry they have, the larger army will always win. Because they can do things the smaller army can't. Like rotate their people so they can get more rest. And performing flanking movements that the smaller army can't. And attacking in greater force.

Greater numbers equal greater power and more options.

And make no mistake about it. When you have something others want, and they are desperate to have it, you are indeed facing a battle situation. To scoff and say you're not is to put your life and the lives of those you love in jeopardy.

To adequately protect your house, you need at least six responsible persons and a communications system.

More about the comm system later. Right now we're focusing on your security team.

Your house is vacant now as far as the neighbors are concerned. But that doesn't mean you're in the clear. There may be a couple of neighbors who saw you moving your cars out of the driveway and parking them down the street. Or that nosy bastard who walks his dog every day and lets him crap in your yard might have seen you moving the porch swing into the back yard.

Or one of your own team may have screwed up and talked too loudly while in the back yard. Or left a light on in the front bedroom one night.

You get the point, I'm sure. We've taken the big target off your house by making it appear vacant, but you still have to set up a security system.

You'll notice I said you need six responsible persons. I didn't say adults. If you have teenagers, and they are reasonably intelligent, they'll make good lookouts.

You'll need to split the team into two. You'll have a daytime team and a nighttime team.

Twelve hour shifts. Hey, we never said this was going to be easy. But the military and some police departments do 12 hours on and 12 hours off for months at a time. If they can do it, you can too.

Besides, there won't be much else to do. It's not like you can just jump in the car and go bowling any more. You won't be going to work once the world turns to chaos, and you won't be going out to eat or to the clubs. Depending on the type of crisis, you'll be stuck at home for as little as a few weeks, or as long as the rest of your natural life.

And, that being the case, there isn't much else to do. So you might as well work twelve hours a day to help pass the time.

Okay, let's go with your daytime team first.

Daytime will be the time when most of the work gets done. The meals get cooked, the drinking water gets boiled, the plants get watered, the schooling gets done, the smaller kids get entertained and the rain water gets collected and processed.

In short, everybody except the three man night shift is up during the day and things run like a regular household. With some modifications.

Your most responsible person needs to be in charge of the day shift. I'm guessing that's you.

Take the other two most responsible people on your shift and position them on guard duty. On the highest floor, on opposite corners of the house.

Remember when we vacated the front rooms to make your house look empty, but we left the blinds down in one front corner of the house? Put one of your lookouts in that room.

By looking out the cracks in the blinds, he can see threats coming from two different directions. Say your house faces north, and the room is on the east side of the house. He can see threats coming from the north or the east. And he can see them in time to send a scramble alert over your communication system (walkie talkies if you can afford them. Short, concise code words if you can't)

The other lookout needs to posted in a room on the opposite corner of the house, so he can see threats coming from the south and west.

The only job for the lookout is to watch. It's not as easy as it sounds, though. It's incredibly monotonous and boring. Especially ten hours into a twelve hour shift. But it's critically important. That's why whoever you put on the windows has to be responsible. You don't want one of them to be taking a nap on the very day that bastard who lets his dog crap in your yard comes to take over your house.

Okay, your lookouts are posted. And, since you're the one in charge, it's up to you to make sure everything else gets done.

Be sure to delegate responsibilities. You don't want to be cooking the meals if your wife is available to do it for you. The kids will be bored out of their minds and will need someone to school them or read to them or play with them. But that doesn't mean you necessarily have to do it.

Delegate. That will free you up to move around throughout the day and make sure everything is being accomplished, spend a little time with your family, and make sure your lookouts aren't slacking off. It'll also enable you to relieve them every hour or so when they need to take a leak or get something to eat or drink.

Within a few days, everyone on your day shift will know their responsibilities and be able to keep themselves busy. And then things will start running smoothly, like a well oiled clock.

Okay, your night shift will consist of three people. There won't be as many activities going on. Most of your group will be sleeping.

Does that mean you can put slackers on your night shift? No. Not at all.

The person in charge of your night shift should be the second most reliable person on your team. If the second most responsible person on your team is your wife, then make it the third most responsible person. It's important to keep you and your wife on the same shift.

One of the people on your night shift, the one in charge, has to be able to think on his feet. The other two have to be good people. They cannot be slackers, because most of your enemies who want to attack you will do so at night.

Your lookouts will spend their entire shifts at their posts, watching for prowlers or any kind of activity. At the first sign of movement, they'll call the third person. The person in charge. He'll come running and assess the threat.

The person in charge will have to make a determination as to the threat level of the situation. In some cases, he may determine that the person the lookout spotted is unarmed and just out scavenging for food or water. If he's considered to be no threat, it may just be a matter of keeping him under surveillance until he's out of sight.

In other cases, if the person is acting suspiciously, or is part of a group, the person in charge may deem it necessary to wake everyone up and move them to the safe room (which we'll teach you how to build in a later chapter).

The person in charge will spend his shift floating back and forth between the lookouts, keeping them on their toes and relieving them occasionally to go to the bathroom, eat, or rest their eyes for a few minutes.

Unlike day shift, where there are a lot of activities going on at once, the sole responsibility of the night shift is security.

A couple of things about the night shift. They have to get used to working completely in the dark. An abandoned house isn't supposed to have any light coming from it. It's permissible to have lights on in some rooms that have the curtains drawn. But the two lookout rooms, the ones on opposite corners of the house where the sentries are posted, cannot have any light at all. Ever.

Not even a lit cigarette.

Make sure you have a quiet room somewhere in the house. A room that is closed off during the day. A room that noisy kids stay away from, that remains closed with the curtains drawn, so that your night shift can get enough sleep each day. Nothing will put you in danger faster than a night shift sentry who is drowsy. You'll have to check on him constantly to make sure he hasn't slumped against the wall and dozed off, or crashed on the floor to take a nap.

And even when he's at his post, watching out the window for movement outside, he's more likely to miss subtle movements in the dark if he's drowsy.

A lookout who is sleepy is not on his game. And that makes him a danger not just for himself, but for the whole group.

20.
Food Prep

Okay, let's talk about food. As in, what kinds of food to buy and store. You've seen all the prepper shows. You've seen all the rich folks buy fancy canning equipment and store hundreds of cans of vegetables.

Now I'm going to try to convince you that they're a bunch of idiots. There's a better way.

Don't get me wrong. If you want to run out and buy two hundred cans of corn, and if you have the money to do so, then who am I to tell you no?

And if you live in a place that has a root cellar, or a basement where it's safe to store canned fruits and vegetables without them freezing in the winter or being ruined by high summer temperatures, then go for it.

I personally have no root cellar and no basement. I wish I did so I could lock my teenage boys in it when they fight. But I don't.

And in case you can't see the folly of buying two hundred cans of corn and setting them aside for the apocalypse, let me explain.

First of all, where are you going to put the two hundred cans of corn? Unless you have a spare bedroom you can devote to food storage, you're probably going to put them in the garage. Am I right?

Uh… but your garage drops below freezing in the winter and can hit a hundred and ten degrees in the summer. And either extreme will ruin all two hundred cans.

And if you're lucky, and the temperature extremes don't get them, time will. They only have a shelf life of eighteen months.

That means that every eighteen months, you'll have to buy two hundred *more* cans to replace them. And you'll either have to throw the original two hundred cans away, or eat corn three times a day for weeks just to keep them from going to waste.

There's a better way. Seriously.

And it's a way that won't kill your budget. Because you don't have to buy a lot of fancy equipment or spend an arm and a leg.

Remember I mentioned before that Sarah and I each spend a small portion of each paycheck for prepping? We do it that way because it's less painful. We can prep without it seeming like we're laying out our life's savings.

We didn't plan it this way, but she almost always spends her prepper money on canned vegetables and potatoes. I almost always spend mine on propane bottles, fresh meat and pasta. And a selected number of canned meats.

Here's the way it works. Sarah will go do her normal grocery shopping on payday. She'll sweep through the store and get everything she needs to feed the family until the following payday. Then she'll go back to the vegetable aisle and see what's on sale. And based on what happens to be on sale, she'll stock up on a certain type.

Say this week, Walmart has their brand name (Great Value) of sweet corn on sale three for a dollar. It's a good price, so she'll buy ten dollars worth.

Now, granted, that's a lot of corn. But we're not going to store it in the garage to get ruined, or store it in the pantry where we'll be scrambling to eat it all before it goes out of date.

No, Sarah is going to dehydrate it.

Okay, I can see the gears turning inside your head. You've seen those rich preppers on TV who spend several hundred dollars buying dehydration machines.

We're not going to do that. Number one, because if I had that much money to throw away on a dehydrating machine, I'd spend it on other, more important things. And number two, it's unnecessary. I'll tell you how you can dehydrate your food without it.

In the summertime, Sarah has me take a folding table from the garage and set it up adjacent to our back deck. And every Saturday during the summer months, she pulls canned goods out of the cupboard. These are the same canned goods she's been collecting every payday for the preceding months.

She has five stainless steel stewpots that she uses for dehydration. (These are the same stewpots we'll use to boil our water and cool our food after the apocalypse, by the way)

She'll start by opening up twelve to fifteen cans of corn. She'll dump them all into a big colander. That's a food drainer with holes in the bottom. Don't feel bad, guys. I had to scratch my head also the first time Sarah called it that.

Anyway, she'll dump the corn into the colander at bedtime so that the next morning every loose drop of water has drained into the sink. It's already on its way to drying out.

When she gets up the following morning, she'll dump the corn into one of the large stew pots. She'll take it outside and put it on the folding table, where it will be in the direct sun all day long.

To keep flies and other insects out of it, she bought five contraptions that look like pot lids, only they're made out what appears to be window screen. It's round, it's covered with stiff metal screen, and it has a plastic handle in the middle.

She says it's actually for steaming vegetables. But it works great for dehydrating food too.

Once the corn is on the table in the back yard, the sun heats up the stainless steel pot and it gets very hot. This speeds up the evaporation process.

We all pitch in together to stir the pot several times a day. Otherwise, the corn on top would dry and the corn beneath it wouldn't.

We stir it first thing in the morning, of course, before we put it out. My daughter Hannah is the first one to get off the bus in the afternoon, and she stirs it again. Sarah goes out after dinner to stir it and we stir it a last time when we bring it in at night.

We thought about leaving it out at night, but Mrs. Willard's cats come into our yard at night when our dogs are locked up and we don't want them to knock the pots off the table or get into them.

I offered to shoot the cats, but Sarah won't let me. Go figure...

Anyway, in the heat of the summer it takes three to four days to turn all those cans of corn into crispy critters. Then Sarah packages it up in airtight containers and puts it away.

As long as it stays dry, it will outlive your great grandchildren. And it'll never lose its nutritional value. When we want to eat it, we just soak it in clean water for a few hours and it's as good as new.

The night after she drains corn in her colander, she'll do the same things with cans of sliced carrots. Or green beans. Or mixed vegetables. The only thing she's found so far that this method doesn't work with is spinach, which for some reason just forms a big nasty clump in the bottom of the stew pot. Like a creature from the black lagoon or something.

Anyway, since she prepares a batch every night, the stew pots are almost always filled during the warm weather months.

As I said, we bring them all inside at night. They continue to dry in the house, just not as quickly.

And she's found that not all vegetables dehydrate at the same rate. Green beans take longer than corn. Sliced carrots dry very quickly. She says it has something to do with the density of the vegetables. I don't know anything about that. I'm just glad this is her project instead of mine.

Sarah dehydrates only those four varieties of canned vegetables in this manner. I asked her why, and she said that those are the only four canned vegetables our family eats besides spinach. She has a point.

However, she also pointed out that dried beans are available in a variety of types and sizes. So is rice and instant mashed potatoes. Last year when we got our income tax refund, we bought a shiny new generator, and enough rice and beans to feed ten people for at least a year.

The vegetables she dehydrates in the back yard merely augment what we already have in our food stores.

She also dehydrates a few fresh vegetables in this manner, though, but mostly as seasoning. Chopped and sliced onions, radishes, and a variety of colored peppers. The first batch she dried out sat in the garage for a couple of months on a shelf. Then one day she made two pots of soup. One had fresh onions, as well as fresh red, green and yellow peppers. The other had similar items that she had dehydrated.

She challenged me to select which was which, and I honestly couldn't.

The only vegetable we've found thus far that can't be dehydrated in this manner (besides spinach, which we can *definitely* live without) are potatoes

Sarah makes the best scalloped potatoes in the western hemisphere. Our family loves them. We don't want to give them up just some day just because the world has descended into chaos. But when she tried to dehydrate them using the sun, they turned black and unappetizing.

. The only fresh fruits we found that we couldn't dehydrate in this manner were sliced apples (because they turn black like the potatoes, and pineapple chunks, because they disintegrate when you stir them.

More about her solution in a minute.

A few more notes about this before we move on to our alternate method of dehydrating foods.

I'd suggest you make this your primary method of dehydrating vegetables for long term storage. It takes very little equipment, and chances are your wife already has some of it. Well, the stew pots, anyway. She probably doesn't have any of those weird screen lid things, but they're only a couple of bucks at Walmart.

In addition to not having to buy a dehydrator, you can do this without jacking up your electric bill. At all. And yes, I know you can buy bags of dried carrots, peas, corn and green beans from one of those survivalist companies. But you'll pay a premium price for them too. Sarah can do it herself for less than half the cost.

And if you're on a budget, like we are, that means we can store twice as much food for the same amount of money. Which means we can live twice as long before we run out. And that's a comforting fact.

We know a couple with a small girl who is seven, I think. Maybe eight. They make up the rest of our team. They're a nice couple, but they're in the same boat we are. Mark and Cinda will come here when the stuff hits the fan. While we are working on the food stores for our own family, they are doing the same thing on their end. We're shooting for three years' worth of food for our family, and Mark and Cinda are shooting for three years for their family.

Once we come together, of course, we all become part of the same family. Instead of our food/their food it will belong to all of us. We will prepare our food as a group and eat as a group. And we will survive as a group.

Okay, vegetables are fine and all that, but I'm a meat and potatoes kind of guy. I can't bear the thought of going four years without meat.

But in a suburban environment, I can't just go out hunting whenever I want. For one, in a society that is starving and desperate, the competition for game will just be too damn fierce.

For another thing, there will be a certain element of the population who considers it easier to steal a dead deer from someone else than to shoot it themselves. Lastly, we're in stealth mode. It's not like I can just drive my pickup up to my front door and download a bunch of venison in my garage without someone noticing.

But the good news is, even if the power is out for a long time, and we have no freezer capability to store meat, we can still have it.

Because meat, it turns out, can be dehydrated too. the process is different, but the result is the same. That's what we'll talk about next.

21.
Processing Meat for the Long Term

I've had a love for hunting since I was seven years old and went out with my dad for the first time. Dad's been gone for several years now, having followed my mom who died just a few months before him.

As for me, I still bring home my white tail every year and usually a good number of ducks and pheasants.

After the apocalypse happens, and I'm confident that it will, I don't expect to have that particular pleasure anymore, and that's an awful shame.

What I expect to happen is that once the grocery stores run out of meat, every yahoo in America with a gun will go the local farmers and take a cow or a pig by force. They'll do the same with commercial stockyards. Before long every farm animal in America will have been slaughtered.

And those who are more honorable, the true hunters of America, will take to the hill country and forests instead. In the absence of packages of hamburger on supermarket shelves, I expect the game population to diminish rapidly.

As for me, I'll let the other fools have it. There will be rank amateurs and novice hunters everywhere, shooting at every rustle of a tree. A lot of them won't know what the hell they're doing, and innocent people will be shot and killed through the carelessness of others.

There will also be those who let someone else track, shoot and clean the kill, and will simply steal it from them at gunpoint.

Me, I'll just stay at home and eat the three years' worth of meat I'll have socked away at the house.

And I'll hope that three years is long enough. That by that time, whatever happened to create such chaos in the world has been fixed, and society is has returned to normal again.

If it hasn't before my three year supply of meat has run out, I guess I'll become a vegetarian. I shudder at the thought.

When Sarah and I started prepping, we set a goal to stock enough food for three years. Our logic was sound. Either society would be back to normal by then and we could get back to a reasonably stable way of life.

Or…

Or by the time our food runs out we'll be good enough at farming our crops to be able to grow them all ourselves.

Yes, I said farming. We'll talk about that in a later chapter, though.

For now, let's get back to meat.

I mentioned before that Sarah spends the warm weather months dehydrating her vegetables and a little bit of fruit.

We live in south Alabama, so we have more warm months than cold ones. But we still have a winter when it gets cold.

That's when she stops doing vegetables and I start doing my meat.

Stop laughing. You know what I mean.

Throughout the year, she and I both watch out for deals on meats. When Walmart or Publix (our local grocer) mark meat down we make sure it's still good. Then we buy it.

As a result, when we go into the winter months, for the last three years in a row, our chest freezer in the garage has been bursting with meat.

We have a second freezer in the garage that is half full of cooked and portioned hot dogs. More on that later. The "hot dog freezer," as Sarah calls it, is where I put the venison and birds I bring home from my hunting trips.

As I write this, it is early November. The weather started getting cold about three weeks ago, and last weekend I began what has become my winter ritual.

On Friday a week ago, I took a five pound venison flank steak and a three pound beef roast out of the freezers and let them thaw. On Saturday morning, I put them both in the oven, and cooked them at 300 degrees. I took a knife and sliced them several times so that the heat could get to every bit of the meat. It's very important that it cook thoroughly. It has to be done before the drying process takes place.

Once both pieces were done, I took them out and let them cool.

I sliced them first into steaks about three quarters of an inch thick. Then I cut each steak into bite sized cubes. When I was done I had a big pile of meat that were three quarters of an inch cubes.

Through trial and error I've found that's just about the right size for dehydrating meat. If it's much larger than that, you run the risk of it not drying completely in the center, and the batch will be spoiled. If it's any smaller, then later on when you reconstitute it into a stew or a soup, it won't even look like meat.

So for my money, three quarters of an inch cubed is just about the right size.

The next part was simple. At bedtime, I spread the meat chunks on cookie sheets and put them back in the oven. This time I set the oven at 175 degrees, and let them dry out all night long.

By morning they had shrunk to about a third of their original size. Before I went to work, I poured them into an airtight container and washed the cookie sheets.

The second night I repeated the process, pouring them out on cookie sheets and baking them overnight at 175 degrees.

Why 175 degrees? Because at that temperature, the meat will dry out without burning.

To be honest, the meat looked dry after the first night. I just repeated the process because I couldn't see the inside of the meat to make sure it wasn't still damp. And after all, it's better to be safe than sorry.

After the second night, I put the meat in gallon sized zip lock bags, and then added it to last year's dehydrated meat in an airtight barrel in the garage. In addition to the meat in the barrel, I've got a couple of FDA-approved absorption packs to absorb any excess moisture. That'll ensure that everything inside the barrel stays dry as a bone.

I'll repeat this process every weekend over the winter months, until I go through all the meat in the freezers.

Besides venison and beef, I've used the same process for duck, pheasant, chicken, turkey and pork. They all work equally well.

I mentioned in my last chapter that Sarah does not dry out potatoes in her big stew pots in the back yard. The first time she tried it, they turned black. I wear the balls in the family, so I put them to use to taste one of the blackened potato chunks.

It tasted like potato, which I guess wasn't too surprising.

But even though the taste didn't appear to be affected, even I had to admit that they didn't look very appetizing. And I'll normally eat anything.

She found that sliced apples did the same thing. And she found that pineapple chunks, although they didn't turn black, turned to mush when she stirred them.

When we found out we couldn't dry spinach in the pots, it was no disaster. Nobody in the family is crazy about spinach.

But potatoes and apples and pineapples were a different matter. We all love them.

Well, Jordan doesn't like pineapples, but he's a bonehead.

My point is that going into the apocalypse without spinach was no big deal. Going into it without apples, potatoes and pineapples is a major crisis.

Our solution was simple.

I share my winter oven usage with Sarah.

As an experiment, Sarah prepared a single cookie sheet to dry in the oven. To fill the cookie sheet she sliced one small potato into slices about a eighth of an inch thick; an apple into wedges, and a small can of drained pineapple chunks.

Everything turned out beautifully. The potatoes look just like the ones in those Betty Crocker scalloped potato boxes on the supermarket shelf. In fact, that's what Sarah plans to do with them. She's dried probably fifty pounds of potatoes in this manner already, and when the time comes she will soak them in warm water to soften them, and then combine them with a variety of seasonings to create several yummy potato dishes.

The pineapples dried quite nicely. Oddly enough, they seemed a lot sweeter (and chewier) when dried. Sarah feels that's because the sugar didn't go away during the drying process. It just got concentrated into a smaller space.

The apple came out nicely too, but for whatever reason took a lot longer to dry out than the potatoes or the pineapples. Go figure…

Since then she's dried peaches, pears, strawberries and kiwis in the same manner. She's not sure if she'll be able to make a decent fruit salad later on after they're reconstituted. But if she can't that's not a problem. We can eat the dried fruit just as it is.

We use the pineapples and most of the apples to make homemade trail mix (more on that later). But some of the apples were set aside for a special purpose. You see, our plan is, while most of the rest of the world is digging in dumpsters looking for scraps of molded bread and stale crackers, we're going to celebrate special occasions… with fresh baked apple pie. (later we'll talk about Dutch ovens and all the neat things you can do with them.)

As I said, this will be the third winter I've done this. Sarah, my lovely wife, occasionally takes some of the dried meat from my barrel to experiment with various dishes. She lets it soak in warm water for several hours (she has to keep it warm because cold water takes considerably longer to soften the meat). Once it softens and expands, she cooks with it.

She has made some awesome stews and soups with the meat, as well as carne guisada (a Mexican dish, essentially beef chunks in brown gravy) and my favorite, chicken chunks in cream gravy.

When the apocalypse hits, everyone else in the neighborhood may be eating their pets or the soles of their shoes. But we'll be eating fairly well.

Should I feel bad about that? Maybe.

But then again, I'm no smarter than any of my neighbors. If I can see ugly things on the horizon, they should be able to see them also. If I take the time and trouble to make preparations for my family and they don't, then that's kinda too bad. I'll feel bad for them. And if I can help them in other ways I will. But I won't share my family's food with people who were too lazy or too short-sighted to prepare.

When I told my friend Tim how I was drying my meat in the oven over the winter months he asked how much it was driving up my electricity bill.

Until that time, to be honest, I hadn't really thought about it.

But it was a valid question, and got me to thinking. I hadn't noticed any big electric bills over the months since I started doing this, so it never raised any red flags. But I got on line and went to my electric company's website. They have a feature where you can compare your electricity usage for that last five years.

I just love the internet, don't you?

Anyway, what I've found surprised me. My using the oven to dry my meats (and some of Sarah's stuff) has had very little affect on our electric bill.

I couldn't understand why until Sarah, who is much smarter than me, explained her theory.

"When you use the oven in the wintertime, it helps heat the house. That means the central heating unit doesn't have to come on as often. It's more or less a trade-off. Whereas if you were using the oven in the summer, it would make the house hotter and make the air conditioner come on more often. *That's* when it would cost us more money on our electricity bill."

In the end, she praised me for choosing to dry my meat in the winter months. She said I was a genius. Which, of course, I already knew.

22.
Wet Versus Dry Foods

As I said before, Sarah and I decided early on that we wanted to store enough food to feed our family for three years. Even though our children are not quite adults, they may as well be. They are all teenagers, and two thirds of them are teenage boys. If you've ever had a teenage boy (or been one), you know that teenage boys are walking, talking garbage disposals. Each of them eat more than I do.

Hannah, our daughter, eats like a bird, though. Averaged out, we figure they equal three adults. Our partners and friends, Tim and Cinda, have a young son. They've also been tasked to provide enough food to feed the three of them for three years.

We have shared our food preparation methods with them, and they've adopted them as well.

Cinda has brought their food over occasionally to store in our garage and attic. After all, when bad things start to happen, they're moving in with us for the duration. At least until the world stabilizes and becomes safe again.

And that's not a bad thing, because Cinda's a real looker. I'm looking forward to seeing her every day (don't tell Sarah I said that, she'll cut my balls off.)

At the present time, Tim and Cinda have about a year and a half's worth of dry food set aside. They're not far behind us.

Not all of your food stores, of course, have to be dry food. We're going with a two to one ratio. When the stuff hits the fan and the world descends into chaos, we'll have roughly one year worth of food in our pantry. It'll be pretty much the same types of food we have now… canned goods, frozen goods, boxed meals, etc.

We've made a few modifications, but not many. And we've done some experiments, like freezing certain types of canned goods so we could thaw them out later to see if they caused problems.

I had to volunteer to be the guinea pig. Sarah refused to, despite my begging her. And she refused to let me experiment on my kids. I thought that was very narrow minded of her.

Anyway, the results of our experiments might surprise you.

Vienna sausages, Spam, Treet and potted meats can be frozen, thawed, and refrozen several times without adversely affecting the product inside the can.

We don't know why this is, but it may be because these products contain little water. The less water in the can, the less it expands when it freezes. In fact, even though many of these cans have pull-top lids, none of them swelled to the point where the lids popped off.

After freezing and thawing twice, I ate each of these products on two different occasions and suffered no ill effects whatsoever.

Armor makes a six pack of Vienna sausages that sells at Walmart for $2.45 and has almost a two year shelf life. Each can, when eaten with four slices of bread or four biscuits, provides more than a third of the daily calories an adult needs to survive.

And, everybody in our family seems to like them.

So Amour Vienna sausages is kind of a no-brainer. We bought fifty of the six packs.

There are several key things to remember when hoarding food. First of all, you don't want to buy more than you can eat before the shelf-life expires. It is insane to buy twenty cans of Ravioli, for example, if you have no plans to eat it. If the crisis doesn't happen before the twenty cans expire, you'll have to throw them away and buy twenty more.

It makes much more sense to buy things you'll eat anyway, rotate it so that you eat the oldest items first, and then replace them as you go.

To explain how this works, let's go back to the fifty six packs of Vienna sausages.

We have a very large walk-in pantry in our house, and the Viennas occupy one corner of the bottom shelf. They have a long shelf-life (almost two years), and when we bought them we took a sharpie and wrote their expiration date on the top of each package.

Then we stacked them so that the ones expiring first were at the top, on the first stack. The newer ones went into the back.

On the shelf above them, Sarah stuck a label that says "Vienna Sausages, 50."

It's a simple reminder that we want to keep fifty of these on hand (more or less) for when the apocalypse hits.

She doesn't make a point to buy one every single time one is used. Mostly because every time she buys some, she has to mark them and pull the whole stack out to put the newer ones in the back.

But she will look at the stack whenever she makes out her shopping list. If we've used four or five of them, she'll restock them.

The Spam and Treet canned lunch meats are kind of a different situation. I'm the only one who likes them. Everybody else just tolerates them.

We stock twenty cans of each, and again, there's a label on the shelf to remind Sarah to replenish them when they drop too far below twenty.

They made it on our list because they meet the same criteria as the Viennas: they can be frozen if we go through a winter without heat, and still be safe to eat; they are fairly high in calories and protein; and they can be prepared in a variety of ways, like on a sandwich, or a biscuit, or just spooned out of a can.

As I said, I'm the only one in the family who likes these particular products. And I don't like them enough to eat twenty cans of each in a year.

So to keep them from expiring before we can replace them with newer ones, we've done two things.

Our kids take their lunches to school, because, well... we're too cheap to buy them. Early in our marriage, we made a point to give the kids lunch money, thinking that school lunches were healthier and therefore worth the extra money.

But those days are over. I mean, the high school cafeteria feeds them things like fish sticks and pizza. The crap they get at school is at least as bad as anything we could send with them.

For our kids, the magic age was ten. We deemed their tenth birthdays as the days when the intelligence fairy came to visit, poured fairy dust over their heads, and made them smart enough to make their own lunches. Ever since then, they've been responsible for making the lunches themselves.

But, because they're teenagers, sometimes they get the lazies. So we gave them an out.

The deal is, they're supposed to make their lunches every night before they go to bed. We don't remind them, because we're trying to teach them responsibility. But at least twice a week, we check the fridge the next morning and see that one of them forgot to make their lunch. Or, in the case of son Zachary, remembered but just didn't want to do it.

No problem. Whenever this happens, Sarah makes the lunch for them. And they get Spam or Treet. So in their own way, they do help me eat it.

And even though they aren't fond of it, when the lights go out and their friends from high school are at home eating the family cat, these guys will be happy to be getting Spam.

Another canned product you might consider stocking a lot of is tuna fish. But not all tuna fish.

The difference in safe and unsafe tuna fish appears to be the brand name, as well as whether or not it's packed in water.

For example, Star-Kist tuna, packed in oil, was fine after being frozen, unthawed, frozen again, unthawed again, then mixed with Miracle Whip and put on a sandwich. I ran the taste test twice on this particular product and had no problems.

However, the same brand, Star-Kist, when packed in water, was a different story.

I froze it and then thawed it the first time, and the can appeared to be unchanged. So I let it sit for a couple of days and froze it again.

This time when I thawed it out I detected a little bit of swelling in the can. It wasn't much, and in fact was barely noticeable. But by comparing the can with another untouched (and unfrozen) can I was able to detect the difference.

The sandwich I ate with this can gave me a stomach ache.

Likewise, both versions of the Walmart brand (Great Value) swelled a little bit when frozen. The one packed in water swelled more than the oil version.

I made a sandwich from each of these cans, but only took one bite from the tuna packed in water. The metallic taste was very noticeable, and I was afraid to go further.

The one packed in oil tasted okay, but my stomach felt a little bit queasy a couple of hours later.

I'm still a tuna advocate. It's high in protein, high in calories when mixed with Miracle Whip or mayonnaise and put on bread, and has a long (eighteen month) shelf life, so you have time to get rid of it before it goes bad.

We've stocked a hundred cans of tuna, but only the one we deemed safe (Star-Kist in oil).

We still haven't figured out the difference between the two. I mean, why one brand gave us problems and the other one didn't. We did notice that the Walmart brand had significantly more water and oil in the cans than the Star-Kist brand did. That may have had something to do with it. After all, more water or oil means greater expansion, right?

In any event, both Miracle Whip and Kraft Mayonnaise can be frozen and then thawed with no adverse impact. I was hoping that only Miracle Whip would be okay, so that a family battle that has waged within this house for years could finally be settled.

My wife, you see, hates Miracle Whip.

Oh, it's not her fault. She was dropped on her head when she was born, and when the doctor picked her up, she slipped out of his hands and fell on her head a second time.

Newborn babies, you see, are quite slippery.

Anyway, I think it was the second bump on her head that made her lose her mind. She actually believes with all her heart that mayonnaise tastes better than Miracle Whip.

I know what you're thinking and I agree with you. I should have her locked up in an asylum somewhere. But I do love her, you see, and she does put out. So I decided to keep her around.

Anyway, I recommend that you stockpile a hundred cans of Star-Kist tuna packed in oil. Don't buy them all at once, though. If you do, they'll all go out of date at the same time. Buy them a few at a time until you get a hundred, and then replace the ones you use on a regular basis. Don't forget to watch the dates and use the oldest ones first.

Oh, and stock about six jars of Miracle Whip also.

We're going to move on to dry stock in a minute, but first, since we're talking about Miracle Whip and mayonnaise, let's get a couple of things out of the way about condiments.

Ketchup and mustard and most pickles do not have to be refrigerated and will last for years under certain circumstances.

First, you must buy them in glass jars, not plastic. Second, you must dip the caps in melted wax (cheese wax, available on the internet for $4.99) and third, you must store it in a cool and dry place. Out of direct sunlight.

When you do need to use it, you'll notice the mustard has turned dark. No problem, it still tastes the same and is safe to eat. The ketchup and mustard will separate, so you'll notice a layer of water on top. Shake it up and that'll take care of it.

The pickles will get softer and softer the longer they're in the vinegar, but they'll still be safe to eat.

Note: There is one brand of pickles (Vlasic, I think) that you'll find in the refrigerated section at your supermarket. That brand does not have preservatives and must be refrigerated. For prepping purposes, pass them by.

23.
Recommended Reading List

Okay, before I forget, I have a list of books I'd recommend you purchase from the Amazon Kindle store. I already priced them. They're only $2.99 apiece, so I know they're within your budget.

The reason I'm recommending them is because I've already read them, and they're all good books for a couple of reasons.

First of all, although they are novels instead of "how to" books, they are about preppers and the things they do to survive a world crisis. In fact, a couple of the ideas I've adopted for my own preparation plans came from some of these books.

But besides the tips you can get from these books, they're also good reading. These four books, more than any other "prepper" novels I've read, capture the essence of the whole prepper culture, and what we'll all have to go through when the time comes and the world descends into a chaotic hell.

I think, and Sarah agrees, that reading such novels helps us to see what it'll actually be like when that time comes. Because through the characters we can actually "live" the experience ahead of time.

We've bought and read a lot of other prepper novels, and if I come across any more worth mentioning, I'll pas it along in the sequel to this book. For now, though, these are my four recommendations:

Countdown to Armageddon by Darrell Maloney. Kindle version: $2.99

Final Dawn: Escape from Armageddon by Darrell Maloney. Kindle version: $2.99

The Prepper Part One: The Collapse by Karl A. D. Brown. Kindle version: $2.99

Dark Days Rough Roads by Matthew D. Clark. Kindle version: $2.99

These are all great books, and worth the money for their informational as well as entertainment value.

A couple more words about books and reading lists…

If you've come across your own recommendations for books that will help others prepare for doomsday, please let me know. I'll mention them on my blog and pass them on in my next book. My email address is *joe50211@yahoo.com*

Second, in one of my later chapters I'll talk about the whole psychological aspect of surviving a doomsday scenario, and how to cope with an endless number of days cooped up in cramped quarters with several other people.

Under extreme situations such as those, it's not uncommon for people to get cabin fever and start to go insane.

We'll talk about various ways to prevent that from happening. And, spoiler alert…

One of the things I'll recommend is that you collect a *lot* of reading material.

Sarah and I have an extra computer, and external hard drive, in our Faraday cage. The hard drive has over two hundred books to read.

In addition, two years ago we gave each of our kids an iPad for Christmas. I have my own, and Sarah has two of them. All of us have loaded them down with books that we purposely haven't read yet.

That's because when the day comes, we can charge the iPads during our daily generator time. And we'll have literally thousands of hours worth of reading time to help us get through those long days.

We'll have other activities too, of course, and we'll talk about them later. But in essence, every book you can store, either in paper or electronic form, will help you and your family in keeping madness at bay. It may not happen this week, or this month, or even this year. But eventually you'll thank me for this little piece of advice.

24.
A Really Cool Recipe

Okay, I'm tired of talking about canned goods and books. Let's talk about pastas and dry beans and other cool stuff.

By the way, I'm sharing a lot of food tips in this volume because Sarah and I have been prepping for awhile, and experimenting for almost as long. We've discovered some things about food preparation that I've never seen anywhere else in any of the other prepper books. Or on any of the prepper shows on television, for that matter.

If I don't share these tips with you, you'll have a much more limited menu. And let's face it. When the chaos comes, we'll have few things to enjoy as it is. We might as well eat some halfway decent food.

In other words, yes, you could survive on rice and beans. But why?

Okay, next up is Kraft Macaroni and Cheese (or a generic equivalent).

Some of you will say, "You can't eat that if the power goes out. It requires margarine and milk."

And if you said that, you'd be wrong.

First of all, this should be one of the staples in your food supply. It is cheap, much tastier than beans, and keeps for years.

Okay, before we go any further, I'll dispel a couple of myths. You *don't* need milk or margarine to make Kraft (or any other brand) of macaroni and cheese.

I know, I know. The recipe is the same regardless of the brand. Boil the noodles for ten minutes or so, then add the cheese mix, a quarter cup of margarine, and a quarter cup of milk.

But here's the thing. You can substitute the milk and margarine with 3/8 cup of Wesson corn oil. For those of you who went to the University of Oklahoma, that's a little bit less than half a cup.

The end result is almost the same. The version made with Wesson oil is a little bit less creamy, and just a little bit more oily. But it's good. And like I said, it beats the hell out of beans and rice.

The other rumor I want to dispel is that the product is no good once it goes past the "use by" date. It just isn't true. Seriously. The box only contains two ingredients. Egg noodles which will outlive you and me and all of our grandkids, and a cheese powder.

The reason for the "use by" date is because even though it's in a foil-lined package, the cheese powder will eventually absorb enough moisture to turn it into a brick.

But that's not a problem. Because all you have to do is lay it on the counter and beat it with your fist or the palm of your hand a few times, and that'll turn it into chunks. Then you add it to the oil and let it sit while the noodles are boiling.

By the time the noodles are finished boiling, the cheese chunks will be soft enough to mix with the oil when you stir it. Then it's a matter of mixing it in the drained noodles and you're done.

We discovered the alternate recipe through trial and error, and as far as I know, we're the only ones who have done so. I've never seen this recipe in any other prepper book.

As for the "use by" date being something to ignore, we tested that theory on a box of macaroni and cheese we found on the top shelf in our pantry when Sarah was in there cleaning. It had fallen over and neither of us had been able to see it. When she found it, she looked at the date, saw that it was six months out of date, and threw it into the garbage.

I'm a cheapskate, so I hate throwing anything away. I saw it on top of the other garbage and took it out and cooked it. It was perfectly fine.

Then we went one step further.

I went to one of those "dollar stores." You know, the ones who are notorious for never rotating their food, and they sell stuff no matter how old it is?

Well, I went in and straight to their shelf of Kraft macaroni and cheese. I moved the first few boxes aside and reached way to the back of the shelf. And there, I was able to find a box that expired two years before.

That's the one I bought. I took it home, cooked it up, and it was perfectly fine.

You'll notice when you make old macaroni and cheese that the cheese, in addition to getting hard, sometimes changes color too. It'll get darker. Don't freak out. It's safe and tastes exactly the same.

The corn oil has an expiration date too. We intentionally used oil that had already expired too. Didn't have any problems with it either. I mean, seriously, what can possibly happen to oil when it gets old? Does it stop being oil? Does it turn into prune juice instead? I've always suspected that expiration dates are mostly just so consumers will throw away perfectly good food and buy new stuff.

Kraft macaroni and cheese is currently selling for 62 cents at Walmart. The Walmart brand, Great Value macaroni and cheese, is currently only 46 cents. In my opinion, Great Value is tastier because it's cheesier. But that's just my opinion.

Anyway, our stockpile contains one hundred boxes of the Great Value brand. We didn't buy them all at once. We bought them a few at a time. And even though we eat them with dinner once a week or so, we replace the ones we use. And the new ones always go to the back of the pile. So when the stuff does hit the fan, most of them will be expired, but not all. And we're not worried about eating the ones which are expired. You shouldn't either.

As for the corn oil, we keep ten bottles of it on hand also.

That's more than we need for the macaroni and cheese, but that's okay. Because we've also stashed bulk popcorn seeds for an occasional treat once the lights go out, to boost morale and provide a cheap snack. And corn oil works great for popping popcorn.

25.
Hot Dogs and Other Cool Stuff

Another thing you might try stocking a lot of is hot dogs. Not the all beef Oscar Meyer kind. They can be way too expensive. Try the cheaper version. They're made of chicken, turkey and pork. But they're still meat, they're high in protein and high in calories. And during a crisis, when some people are resorting to eating bugs, no one in your group will complain that they aren't good enough. I guarantee it.

We buy the Bar-K brand, sold at Walmart for 88 cents a pack (Have you ever noticed that Walmart has a fetish for the number 8?) Anyway, I've already told you that I spend part of my weekly prepper budget on meats. A lot of what I buy is hot dogs, and yes, hot dogs count as meat. Maybe not the choicest kind of meat there is, but like I said, it's protein and it's calories. And you'll need both to survive.

I buy the hot dogs eight or ten packages at a time. Even though the package says they're fully cooked, I just can't stomach a cold dog right out of the package (and I'll eat pretty much anything).

So I take those eight or ten packages of hot dogs home and I put them in one of Sarah's big stew pots. I fill it half full of water and I let them simmer for awhile. Then I drain the water and let them cool.

Walmart sells these little zip lock bags for school lunches and such. They're called "snack size," and they're about half the size of a regular sandwich bag.

They come 100 bags to a box, for a couple of bucks.

After the hot dogs cool, I bag them in the snack sized bags, two hot dogs to a bag.

Then I stack them nice and neat on the bottom of my second chest freezer. I've got at least a thousand of them there now, packaged in pairs, waiting for the day when someone will free them from their cold and lonely prison and eat them.

I know you've got several questions. Like, why hot dogs? We've already covered that. They're cheap, and they're high in both protein and calories. A perfect prepper food.

Why package them two at a time?

If whatever crisis befalls the country happens to happen in the winter time, and if the power grid goes down, all of your food is going to freeze. These hot dogs will already be frozen, so that doesn't matter.

However, under those circumstances, all food will have to be thawed before it's eaten.

Under those same circumstances, you and your group will dress in layers to stay warm. You will probably wear two of three shirts as well as a jacket.

To conserve heating fuel, all you have to do is issue two or three packages of hot dogs to each of your people and tell them, "This is your meat ration for tomorrow."

They will tuck the first two shirts into their pants, and place the hot dogs between the next layer before tucking that in. The hot dogs will ride around under their coat overnight and thaw. They won't be directly against the person's skin, and won't cause frostbite. And if it makes one spot so cold it becomes uncomfortable, they can easily shift it to another spot.

The next day, after the hot dogs are thawed, they can eat their meat ration at their own leisure (for you people from Texas, that means whenever you want).

Another option is just to drop the hot dogs inside the sleeve of your coat. The heat from your arm will eventually thaw the dogs, but it takes a little longer.

If by chance, the power grid goes down in the summertime, when it's hot, don't worry. We have a solution for that too.

If that happens, you'll be on a cooking frenzy, trying to cook as much stuff in your freezer as you can before it spoils. Cooked food lasts much longer, you see.

But you don't have to worry about the hot dogs. Save the fire for the chicken and roasts you're cooking. Let mother nature take care of the hot dogs for you.

All you have to do is slice each of the hot dogs up into ten or so bite sized pieces. Then dump them all into one of those big stainless steel stew pots, cover the top with the screen to keep the bugs out, and set it in the sun. Just like you dried out all of those vegetables, remember?

We actually did this to some hotdogs last summer to try it out.

What we found was it takes a little bit longer to dry out hot dogs than it takes to dry out vegetables.

No, I don't know why. It just does.

It took three days instead of two. No big deal, really.

Once they were dry, they had a little bit of an oily feel to them. Also no big deal. It's just because of the high fat content, and oil doesn't evaporate like water does.

Once you do this, the hotdogs are shelf-stable, which means they no longer have to be refrigerated or frozen. And they, like the other stuff you dehydrated, will last for years.

To test the ones we dried out, I put my test batch in a bowl, and let it sit on the back of our kitchen counter for about three weeks or so.

Then one day I was in the kitchen looking for a snack, and grabbed a handful.

They weren't prime rib, but they weren't bad, either. I was so impressed that I made another batch the same way with about twenty packages of hot dogs. Those are now stored with the rest of our dry stock.

We've also stocked quite a bit of beef jerky in our dry stock. Beef jerky is ridiculously easy to make.

In fact, I've already pretty much told you how.

Up to this point, all of the information I've shared with you about dehydrating meat in the oven pertained to unseasoned meats. They're unseasoned because I don't have a clue what Sarah will do with them when the time comes. She'll mix some of them with gravies or sauces of various types. Others she'll make into stews.

But here's the thing… jerky is made the same way. Just take cooked beef, heavily seasoned with salt and pepper or other spices, cut it into thin strips, similar to bacon, and dry it out in the oven. Make sure the heat is low, around 175 degrees, so it doesn't burn.

Once it's dried sufficiently, pack it away.

26.
The Importance of Counting Calories

Let's take a break from food preparation for a minute to talk about counting calories.

I told you before that Sarah and I plan to have enough food put away to feed us all for a period of three years.

I should have elaborated on it then, but I didn't, and some of you may have asked the question, "But how do you know when you've got enough for three years?"

The answer is easy. You don't count packages. You count calories.

Cinda used to be a math teacher. She's good at this. She explained it to me not long ago, and I was able to understand it, even though I hated math in school. Still do. And to this day I think math is overrated. I mean, when was the last time anybody asked you to do algebra? For me that answer is never.

Anyway, scientists cannot agree on how many calories a human body needs stay healthy. The estimates range from 1500 calories a day for people who mostly just sit around all day, to 2400 calories a day, for people who work hard all day.

That's a wide range.

During the apocalypse, we'll be doing mostly the sitting around part, but also some standing (guard duty) and light chores (gathering firewood, cooking, etc.)

So we figured 1800 calories as a starting point. Then, knowing that the human body burns calories faster when it's cold (to stay warm), we factored in another 200 calories a day. That way if the power grid goes down and we have no heat in the winter months, we're covered. In the summer months, the extra 200 calories will give us the extra boost of energy we need to chop down trees, plant and care for crops, and go on resupply runs to collect anything we need.

Okay, that brings our starting point to 2000 calories per day, per person.

If you take 2000 calories and multiply it by eight (people in our group), we need 16,000 calories per day. Multiply that by the number of days in three years (1095), and you have the total number of calories we'll need for all eight of us to survive for three years.

For us, the magic number is 17,520,000 calories.

Now, Seventeen and a half million calories sounds like a lot, and it is. But here's the thing. It adds up a lot faster than you think it does.

When I said count by the calories, not by the package, this is what I meant:

I could go into our pantry and see a hundred boxes of macaroni and cheese, fifty six packs of Vienna sausages, eighty cans of spaghetti sauce, forty boxes of spaghetti noodles, and all the other crap we have in there. And I could say, "Yeah, that looks like about three years' worth. We can stop now."

But it would be nothing but a wild add guess. And it might be wrong. And we could die of starvation because of my stupidity.

On the other hand, if I took the time to look at each item and read the nutritional information on the boxes, I'd see that box of macaroni and cheese contained three servings of 250 calories each. I'd multiply 250 by three and know that the box contained about 750 calories. The hundred boxes therefore contain about 75,000 calories. So we can subtract that from the 17,520,000 that we need.

The spaghetti noodles in our pantry each have ten servings of 210 calories. That's 2100 calories per box, times forty boxes equals 84,000 calories. So we subtract that from the 17, 520,000 total as well.

Now, some of it is guesswork. Since we plan to make our macaroni and cheese with corn oil instead of milk and margarine, we have to modify the number of calories per box slightly. But you get the idea.

And for the record: Yes, I know this is a pain in the ass. That's why I'm glad that Sarah and Cinda are doing it instead of Tim and me. We'd screw it up big time.

That, in a nutshell, is how you make sure that if you plan to have three year's worth of food, you really do.

Early on in this process, I hung a small whiteboard in our garage. It's one of those boards you can use dry erase markers on. I stole it from the office supply closet. Shhh. Don't tell anybody.

Sarah took a dry erase marker and wrote 17, 520,000 on the board in big red letters. That was our goal. And ever since then, every time we've prepared a new batch of dried vegetables, or dried meat, or added forty boxes of this or that into the pantry, she's computed the number of calories we've thrown into the pile, and subtracted that number from the total.

Tim and Cinda live about four miles away from us. It's close enough to walk to us if they have to. One of the books I recommended, *Countdown to Armageddon*, talks about what would happen if there were severe solar storms and the earth was bombarded with electromagnetic pulses (EMPs). Basically, every vehicle on earth would instantly die, and would never start again, unless all of the electrical components were replaced with new ones. That's what we (Me, Sarah, Tim and Cinda) believe is most likely to happen.

Anyway, like I said, four miles is close enough to walk to our house if and when that happens. They have backpacks ready to go with water and snacks, and they already have some of their clothes stored at our place.

But on foot, they cannot bring mass quantities of food with them.

So every weekend, for the last year and a half, Tim and Cinda have stopped by our house to visit. And while they're here, we unload whatever dry stock and pantry items they want to add to our food stores.

Since Cinda used to teach math, she's always got the calculations done, and we merely subtract her calorie count from the number on our white board.

It works quite well.

And like I said, seventeen and a half million looks like a daunting number. But when you consider that every time you subtract from it, you're talking about numbers in the thousands, it makes that big number seem a bit more manageable.

Now, the next logical question you're asking is "What about the intangibles? The odds and ends that don't have a package to tell me how many calories are in it?"

Good question. It's obvious you're paying attention.

You're talking about things like the potatoes that Sarah slices up and puts into the oven to dry. Or the flour that she's putting aside to bake bread with. That kind of stuff, right?

This part's easy too. Just go on the internet and buy a calorie count book. Or better yet, some sites have charts that you can just print out. It'll have damn near everything. Those charts have more food than a stripper has high heels. Whatever food you plan to stock, it's on those charts somewhere.

For example, it might say that a cup of sliced bananas is 100 calories. Fine. There's your answer for a food that doesn't come with a label.

But be careful, and here's why:

It's talking about a cup full of raw bananas. If you take that same cup of bananas and slice them into banana chips and then dry them in your oven, they'll shrink to about half their size. But they'll retain the same number of calories. So then half a cup of dried bananas will equal 100 calories.

The bottom line is this… always compute your calories with foods in their natural form.

Another hint. We struggled early on how much of a fudge factor to build in. To account for any losses we might incur to our food store.

You know, in case Sarah ever burns a big pot of stew and it has to be dumped out.

Or someone drops a bag of flour and it explodes and goes everywhere.

At first we figured we'd just add another 50,000 calories in ahead of time, to cover for those kinds of things.

But then Sarah had a much better idea. She now makes her own trail mix. It looks a lot like the stuff you can buy in the package for $4.88 at Walmart (They really do have a fetish for the number 8).

But Sarah's version is much cheaper. We'll talk about how she makes it in the next chapter.

For now, though, I'll just tell you her plan.

The whole family loves her trail mix, so she makes a lot of it. And once she makes it, she seals it up in airtight buckets and puts them in the garage. We've got a lot of it out there. Probably more than we'll ever need. But that's okay, because trail mix is very high in calories. And we don't include the calories in our calorie count. These calories are off the books.

If we ever burn a pot of stew or break a bag of flour, no problem. we just give everybody a couple of handfuls of trail mix and that makes it all better. And it covers for the loss.

Plus, if anybody is ever tasked to take a long journey or do something really strenuous, we can give them extra rations (trail mix) to keep their energy level up without lessening the calorie count for everybody else.

Plus, if we ever need something we don't have, and are in a position to barter for it, we figure that trail mix is one of the two best things to barter with.

I'll reveal the second thing later on. It will surprise and amaze you, and you'll wonder why you never thought of it. In the meantime, you can guess.

Trail mix might seem like a strange thing to barter with, but I'll guarantee you this. If a man has been eating rice and mice for three straight months to survive, and you show him a container full of trail mix with nuts and apple chunks and M&Ms in it. His eyes will get as big as saucers. His mouth will water so much he'll look like a rabid dog. And he'll give you whatever you want.

Now, it's not that I don't trust Sarah's judgment. I really do. After all, she's way smarter than I'll ever be.

But the truth of the matter is, I'm way more cautious than she is.

That's why, when we decided to make the trail mix our "fudge factor," I went a little bit further.

I purposely didn't subtract the calories for several batches of dried meats I took out to the garage.

Call me crazy, but I like the thought of having a little extra cushion to mess around with.

But do me a favor and don't tell Sarah. She'll kick my ass.

27.
Something Better Than Gold

Okay. On to Sarah's recipe for trail mix. It's great because, number one, it lasts forever. I've eaten it when it was two years old, and it still tastes great.

The marshmallows are a little bit chewy by then, and the M&Ms aren't fresh any more.

But that's minor. Even two years old it tastes great and satisfies my sweet tooth. And more importantly, it adds a lot of calories to my diet.

As I said before, you can purchase trail mix by the bag at the supermarket. And if we were a rich family, we'd have done that, just to save ourselves the trouble.

But we're not rich. We're an average middle class family with a mortgage and two car payments, trying to save enough money to put three kids through college.

And we're definitely on a budget.

So we choose to make our own trail mix at about half the cost of the prepackaged version.

Sarah has this big glass bowl. It's fancy and etched with foo-foo designs and flowers and stuff. She had it when we got married many years ago, so I'm not even where it came from. It looks like a punch bowl you see at a wedding reception. And it's as big as my sister's ass.

That's pretty big.

Anyway, when she goes grocery shopping occasionally, she'll use her prepper funds to buy the four main parts of the trail mix: salted cashews, honey roasted peanuts, marshmallow bits (the tiny ones) and raisins.

Those are the standard items, the ones that are always in the trail mix.

She'll also get either M&Ms, Reese's Pieces, or jelly beans so she can make each batch a little bit different and they're not always the same.

Lastly, she'll take some of the pineapple chunks and apple slices we've dried out at the house. They're pretty good size, so she'll cut them into smaller pieces.

Then she throws all this stuff into her glass bowl, stirs it all up by hand, and abracadabra! She's got a whole bunch of trail mix.

Let me insert a quick note here.

Another good thing about making your own trail mix is that you can modify it to your own desires. If you don't like Reese's Pieces, you can insert something else instead. Or just leave the suckers out. If you don't like roasted peanuts, you can sub them with pecans or walnuts. That way you won't have to pick them out and give them to the kids later on.

I don't have a big sweet tooth, but I love Hot Tamales candy. I don't know why, I'm not a psychiatrist. And no, I didn't sleep with my mother. I just like them, okay?

Anyway, Sarah announced one day that while I was hunting, she made two big batches of trail mix. She said for the candy item she used Hot Tamales instead of M&Ms. I said, "Great! Where are they? I'll sample them and let you know how good they are."

But she wouldn't tell me. She knows I'll eat the whole batch. She knows me pretty well.

When the shit hits the fan, and the world is going crazy, and we're surviving on 2000 calories a day, the only thing that'll keep me going is knowing eventually we'll come across that trail mix with the Hot Tamales.

When she finishes a batch, she gets out a calculator and does some computations to get a rough estimate on how many calories a cup of the stuff contains. It varies, based on the ingredients. It's usually between 350 and 450 calories per cup.

Remember those snack sized zip-lock bags we put the cooked hot dogs in?

She takes some of those, and a sharpie, and writes "350" or "410" or whatever the calorie count is. Then she measures out one cup per bag, until the bowl is empty. She takes the bags and puts them in an airtight container in the garage. But she doesn't subtract the number of calories from the total number we need on the white board.

These calories are a freebie.

Okay, I'm going to go off topic again, but this is important, so please take note.

There are a lot of differing opinions on exactly what crisis is going to befall the world (or this country) in the coming years.

For my money, I'm betting that we're overdue for a series of bad solar storms that are going to short out everything electric and electronic.

If I'm right, then anything you don't protect inside a Faraday cage or box will be worthless. And that includes your entire house's electrical system.

If that happens, it will take a very long time to recover. And in the meantime you'll have to survive winters with no heat and no electricity, unless you had the foresight to protect heaters and a generator in a Faraday cage.

So, let's say you didn't do that. Or maybe you did, but it's so damn cold that the little heaters you're running off the generator just won't do the trick.

Staying warm under such conditions isn't the only problem you'll have. Bringing a pot of water to boil when it's twenty degrees outside takes *five times* the amount of fuel or firewood as it takes to boil the same water when it's eighty degrees outside.

There will be some days when it just makes no sense to cook. Or you'll want to, but won't be able to because doing so will exhaust your supply of wood or fuel.

In those cases, things like hot dogs packed two to a bag, bread slices packed two to a bag, or trail mix come in very handy.

Say it's twenty degrees outside. You're low on wood so you can't cook. All you have to do is give each of your people two packs of hot dogs, two packs of sliced bread, and two packs of trail mix.

That's their full allotment of calories for the day. They can pack them inside their clothing to thaw and warm them to body temperature. Then they can eat them throughout the say whenever they want.

And all of you will be warmer on such days. Because instead of trying to keep a fire going to cook your meals, you can huddle in the safe room around the heater riding out the cold snap.

28.
Baking While Roughing It

A few months ago Sarah told me she was going to stock forty five-pound bags of flour, and asked me for advice on how to store them.

I asked her why in the world we needed forty bags of flour. I said I liked tortillas, but not every single day. And I'll eat hard tack, but only if I'm pretty damn hungry.

She gave me a "duh" face and said, "I'm going to bake our bread."

Sometimes Sarah doesn't understand guy things. Like how many electrical items you can run off a 2000 watt generator.

I explained that the typical heating element in an electric oven draws about 3000 amps.

I went on to explain that the generator only supplies 2000 amps. And that's if it's not powering anything else.

I couldn't resist being a smart ass. Because it's not very often I think I know something she doesn't. So I pushed my luck and said, "And 3000 is bigger than 2000. So your evil plan will not work, honey."

She looked at me and bit her lip for a moment. Then she said, "Oh ye, of little faith."

I got the distinct impression she wanted to say something a bit more... colorful.

Five minutes later she called me from the bedroom.

I thought oh, boy. Because the kids weren't due to be home for another hour. And because makeup sex is the best kind.

But that's not what she wanted. She was sitting in front of our computer, which is in the bedroom.

She said, "Check this out, smartass."

And she showed me a charcoal powered oven she'd ordered on eBay.

Now, I didn't even know such a thing existed. But after I looked at the photos and read the description, I was impressed.

The charcoal oven is about the size and shape of a microwave oven. Only it doesn't plug into the wall. It has a tray on the bottom that comes out so you can fill it with charcoal.

The bottom of the oven is thin metal, which transfers the heat into the cooking compartment. The cooking compartment is insulated, so the heat stays inside the compartment. It has a glass door with a small thermometer on the inside of the glass to show you what temperature your food is cooking at.

The charcoal tray has a crank so it can be lowered up to three inches, to move it farther away from the cooking compartment if your food is getting too hot. That's how you regulate the temperature.

Once I saw it, I thought it was the greatest thing ever. I wish I had invented it.

She paid $179 bucks for it, from our tax refund money. And, it turned out, there are cheaper options. Coleman offers a different version that burns propane, for only $49. It's smaller, though, and would only bake one loaf of bread at a time.

I'm happy with the one we have. Sarah has already experimented with it, and went through a few loaves that were either too crunchy or too doughy. Now, though, she's an expert. The bread she's able to bake is easily as good as store bought, and almost certainly healthier too, since it doesn't have any of the preservatives.

We bought twenty bags of charcoal and stacked them in the garage behind the Faraday cage. They're out of the way, there. And they never go bad.

She took eight loaves of her bread and sliced them on her manual bread slicer ($14.88 at Walmart.com). She put two slices each in a whole bunch of ziplock sandwich bags. Then she stacked them on top of all the hot dog packs in the freezer in the garage.

I asked her what she'd do with them if the power grid went down in the summertime, and we had to use the bread slices quickly.

She said, "While you're slicing up and drying the hot dogs, I'll be making potato bread soup and bread stuffing with chicken chunks."

Yummy.

29.
How to Stockpile Medicines

I take Vasotec to help control my high blood pressure. I've always had a problem with my blood pressure being too high. But hey, it's my only flaw. Otherwise I'm perfect. So it's okay.

Sarah is standing behind me, reading over my shoulder.

She's shaking her head.

Okay, she's gone now.

Bitch.

No, actually, she's a sweetheart and the love of my life.

Please don't tell her I called her a bitch. She'll kick my ass.

Anyway, the point I'm trying to make is that I, like millions of other Americans and people of lesser countries, take prescription drugs. I'll bet someone in your group does too.

Prescription drugs have always been a big problem for preppers, because it's not something you can hoard. And you can't just go out and buy a truckload of them either when you sense that doomsday is drawing near.

And lastly, they are a problem because most prescription drugs have a shelf life of only a few months or a year. If you're holed up in your house for two years waiting for society to return to normal again, that could be an issue.

Here's a glimmer of hope: The American Medical Association did a study not long ago. They determined that the reason prescriptions for medications have increased tenfold over the last generation is because they are way overprescribed.

Bear in mind that this is an organization of doctors. And even they are saying that a lot of doctors (most, in fact) prescribe meds way more than they should.

The AMA says that in a lot of cases, our ailments don't really need powerful medications. They can be treated in other ways. Like a change of lifestyle, or more exercise, or a healthier diet.

I consider that good news for preppers.

Because it means that if we are holed up for a long period of time and cannot get our medications, it doesn't necessarily mean a death sentence when we eventually run out.

Okay, having said that, I've got two suggestions to help the situation ahead of you.

Here's the first one:

About two years ago, Walgreen's started offering an option of getting your refills for ninety days instead of thirty. Now, on the face of it, that sounds like a good idea. I mean, why go by there once a month if you can go every three months, right?

But I said, "no thanks."

The reason I did that is because my health plan approves refills up to four days in advance. And the more often I refill my prescription, the more extra medicine I can stockpile for a doomsday scenario.

I'll bet your health plan does the same thing. It may not be four days, it may be three. Or it may be five. But I'll bet that it lets you get a refill while you still have a few pills left in the old bottle.

Here's why that's important.

Say you see your doctor and he writes you a prescription for a month's medication, with two refills. He tells you to come back and see him when you pick up the last of the refills.

So, you look at the calendar and it's January 20th.

You rush over to Walgreen's and get your first month's supply.

And the next month, you go back for a refill on February 16th, not the 20th.

If you have the same health plan I do, Walgreen's will call it in and they'll approve it. Because four days is close enough. They'll figure maybe you're going to be out of town on the 20th, or maybe in jail or something. So they say sure, the 16th is close enough.

And then the following month, in March, you pick up the final prescription on the 12th.

Well, that's your last bottle. So you need to see the doctor again.

When you call for the appointment, tell the receptionist that April is going to be a very busy day for you. The only day you can possibly come in will be the 8th.

And then on April 8th, after you see the doctor and get the prescription renewed, you high-tail it back to Walgreens to pick up your first month's supply.

You get the idea. And this works. Like I said, I've been doing it for a couple of years now and I've got an extra two month supply in the medicine cabinet.

Here's another tip.

If you get any advance notice that doomsday is upon us, like if you're watching TV and they say a meteorite is going to collide with the earth next week,

Or if the Air Force says four of their nuclear weapons were stolen and they suspect they're in the hands of terrorists,

Or (my scenario of choice) they announce that there are a series of violent solar storms on the surface of the sun,

Or, if a race or class or ethnic war starts and there are riots in the streets of many U.S. cities...

If any of those things happen, go to Walgreens. Tell them you want to switch to their ninety day plan.

They'll have to call the doctor, of course, to get his okay.

Once the doctor gives his approval, the health care provider will also. They may insist on calling the doctor to verify his decision, but they won't question it.

After all, they know they'll have to give you the meds eventually anyway, right?

Ideally, if you start socking away extra meds now, and if you're able to get another ninety day supply before you go to ground, you may have as much as a six month supply when the trouble starts.

Depending on the nature of the crisis, that may be enough. Society may be back to normal within six months.

And if it's not, we'll talk about that in the next chapter.

By the way, if you are able to stockpile extra medication, make sure you keep track of which bottles are oldest. Medicines tend to have a short shelf life, so you'll always need to take the oldest ones first.

And keep your extras in the freezer. For most meds, it'll extend their life.

30.
When Your Medicine Runs Low

Okay, back to the prescription drug issue. Hopefully when you hunker down to sweat out the storm, you have a supply of meds that will last you several months.

You have a very big decision to make. And it won't be an easy one.

Your choices will basically be:

a: Do I take the dosages prescribed on the bottle and hope like hell I can get more before I run out?

b: Do I start to change my lifestyle as much as I can, so I can wean myself off of the drugs? That way when I do run out it won't be such a shock to my system when I quit cold turkey.

As I said, it won't be an easy decision, and I don't envy you for having to make it.

As for me, I've already decided what I'm going to do.

I'm going to reduce my medication by half. Take one pill instead of two. Then I'm going to relax as much as possible, take a nap every day, and try not to get stressed.

If I feel lightheaded or dizzy, or particularly out of sorts, I'll take another pill to see if it helps. But mostly, I'll try to get by on half of my prescribed dosage.

Because then my medicine will last twice as long.

Let me give you another example, so you'll understand what I mean by lifestyle change.

I'm not a diabetic. My father was, though, so I know that sometimes it's treated with prescription medicine.

If I were a diabetic when doomsday hit, I would reduce my dosage by half, and go on a strict no sugar, very low carbohydrate diet. I would rest throughout the day, try to get more exercise, and be sure I drank plenty of water.

And I would cross my fingers and pray a lot.

Remember the AMA study that said doctors way overprescribe meds. I took that to mean that many, or most of us, can really get by without them if we just make some changes to our lives.

Ideally, we'll never find out because we'll never be in a situation where meds are not available.

But if that time ever does arrive, at least you'll have some options.

31.
Don't Overlook Your Trees

I grew up in a poor family, and as a result I've been rather thrifty my whole life. I'm always looking for ways to save a few dollars here and there.

My wife prefers to call me a cheapskate. But in the end, it boils down to pretty much the same thing.

Since I'm so thrifty/cheap, I've always wondered why people plant trees that offer them nothing in return.

As I walk around my neighborhood, I see plenty of spruce trees, and a few maples. Here and there is an oak tree.

But I seldom encounter an apple, or a peach, or a pecan tree, even though the soil here in south Alabama is rich enough for any of them to thrive.

In fact, I've planted a lot of trees since I moved out on my own. I have never, ever planted a single tree that didn't bear some kind of fruit or nut.

Even before I was a prepper, we had a pecan tree and an apple tree in our back yard. Both of them have root systems that are established enough so that we very seldom have to water them. If fact, I can count on one hand the times I've had to water them in the last five years. Basically when we were on the verge of drought conditions and hadn't had any significant rainfall in a couple of months.

Sarah and I went to the home of one of her co-workers across town about a year and a half ago. They were having a barbeque. As we sat on lawn chairs in their back yard, I marveled at an orange tree they had. It seemed to be thriving, and had at least a hundred oranges on it.

I never knew you could grow oranges in south Alabama, but it turns out you can. I also found out that orange trees have a fairly deep root system, so once their roots are established (by their third year), they don't require constant watering.

I asked if there was any chance of losing the crop to a freeze, and they said they'd never lost one. The oranges don't show up on the tree until the blossoms fall off in the spring. And they're ripe enough to harvest in late summer.

Within a week, I had an orange tree just like theirs in the corner of my back yard. It was a yearling, and it's been in the ground for a year and a half now, so it's pretty close to getting its roots established.

This past year we even got six oranges off of it. Granted, that's not many, but it's supposed to double each year until it reaches maturity. Then it'll produce eighty to a hundred oranges a year.

I have to say it was pretty cool, growing our own oranges.

We also get apples from our apple tree and pecans from our pecan tree.

Sarah's trying to convince me to add a peach tree, but I've resisted her efforts thus far because too many trees will reduce our rain catching ability. We have to leave a certain amount of the yard to roll out our rain tarps.

Besides, I hate peaches.

My point is this…

We don't know when the trouble is coming. It might come next week.

Or, it might come three years from now.

But whenever it comes, if you have the capability of growing some of your own fruits and nuts, it will go a long way to stretching your food supply.

And, it'll give you something else to barter with.

I'd recommend you at least consider the feasibility of planting some fruit bearing trees in your back yard. Which ones will of course depend on what grows well in your area. And when you place them, be sure you don't place them so close to your fence that it interferes with your rain catching operation. Or so close to your house that it clogs your rain gutters with leaves.

If you live in a relatively rainy climate, you might also consider a few grape plants. Grapes are cool things to have for several reasons. First of all, they take up very little space if you plant them in a sunny spot next to your fence and train the vines to climb the fence.

Second, they can produce an awful lot of grapes, and don't go to waste. If they produce more than you want to eat, merely harvest them and turn them into raisins.

The only problem is that they have shallow root systems, and are almost all liquid. They require a good bit of water. If you live in a dry climate, this won't be an option for you.

32.
Do You Need a Hot Box?

Obviously, since none of us really know what form doomsday is going to take, we have to prepare for the worst. By that, I mean we don't know what's going to happen. So just to be on the safe side, we have to assume it's going to last longer than the three years we have food for.

In other words, we have to plan for what we'll do when we run out of food.

For this part of the book, I'm going to have to credit Darrell Maloney, because I got this idea directly from his book *Final Dawn: Escape From Armageddon.*

That's one of the books I suggested you read in an earlier chapter, and the reason I have to credit him is because I had planned to stock seeds to use when we ran out of food. But I didn't put any further thought into it than that.

When I read that book, and when I saw how his characters kept their seeds fresh for seven long years, it made me think. Seeds only last a year or two. If I didn't modify my plans for storing my seeds, they would probably be worthless when the time came to use them. So here's my modified plans for my seeds.

As I said, seeds only last for a couple of years. Theoretically, you can freeze them and they'll still be good for longer than that. But if the power grid is down, you cannot maintain freeze temperatures over the summer months.

I explained this dilemma to Sarah, who explained it to Cinda, and the two of them did some extensive research on the internet. And what they decided we needed to solve our problem was kind of a miniature greenhouse, or a "hot box."

Here's the good news. First of all, we priced the materials for a hot box, and can build one for less than a hundred dollars easy. Second, not everybody will need one. In fact, where we live in southern Alabama, we don't even think we'll need it. But we designed it and stocked the materials anyway, just in case.

A hot box is simply a miniature greenhouse, and its purpose is to take your existing growing season and to extend it by four months.

Say, for example you live in Michigan.

Normally your last freeze comes in April, or maybe early May. Your first freeze is usually around the first week in October.

A hot box allows you the option of planting your crops a bit earlier. Say, February, for example. And you may not have to harvest them until, say, late November or early December.

And that's important, because you might have enough of a growing season to plant a single crop and harvest it without the hot box.

But having the hotbox will allow you to grow an early crop, let it mature and harvest it, and then plant a second crop to be harvested before winter.

Seeds are going to be a precious commodity once the apocalypse hits. Because it's your food source for the future.

Since the seeds don't last very long, you'll have to use some of your seeds to actually grow plants each spring. Even while you're hunkered down in "stealth mode." Then, you'll use the new seeds you get to replace your old ones.

Here's how it works. Say you're not very finicky about your food. You figure you and your family can survive on beans and corn for the rest of your lives. And, you're the guy who lives in Michigan. You won't need a hot box, because the amount of crops you have to grow each year is minimal.

In your case, you simply plant one third of your seeds in the springtime the first year after the apocalypse hits. You care for them, and water them, and grow them to maturity. And then you harvest them, package the seeds, mark them with the date, and they become your new seeds.

The next season, you use another third of your old seeds and do the same thing.

Why a third, instead of all of them?

Because if you plant all of them, and you have a late freeze you didn't expect, or a very heavy rainstorm, you'll lose the whole crop.

If you plant a third, and you lose the crop, you'll be able to use a second third to replant, and still have enough seeds to replant the next year

Obviously, you'll do the same thing with your corn crop. Grow the corn plants right next to your beans, using a third of your seeds per year.

And by replacing your old seeds with new ones each year, when the time comes to break out of your house and start farming your crops on a large scale, you'll have seeds that actually work.

But, say you're that guy in Michigan, but you *don't* want to be restricted to beans and corn for the rest of your natural life.

No problem. Just build yourself a hot box as we describe in a minute. Then plant your beans and corn each year while you're hunkered down. Start whenever the hot box has been above fifty five degrees for six straight days. It'll probably be late February or early March.

Care for your crops and water them and stuff. On warm days, keep the door open so the bees can get in there and pollinate the plants. And when they mature, harvest them, pull up the plants by the roots, and immediately plant your second crop.

Your second crop can be anything you want. Different kinds of beans, a few stalks of wheat, strawberries, squashes, whatever.

Remember, you don't need to plant a whole bunch of everything. All you need is three or four plants of each thing to harvest the seeds. You're not trying to feed yourself at this point. Only to ensure you have fresh seeds when you come out of hiding.

The hot box should allow your second crop time to grow and mature so that you can harvest it before winter temperatures roll around again.

Okay, say you don't live in Michigan. Say you live in southern California, or Florida.

If that's the case, you obviously won't need a hot box.

You will have to plant a third of your seeds each year, though, so you can harvest new seeds and keep them fresh.

As for me, where I live we have a long growing season, and I could probably squeeze in two sets of crops each year.

But also where I live, we sometimes get heavy rains from hurricanes that strike either the east coast of Florida and sweep across us, or actually enter into Gulf of Mexico waters and hit Louisiana.

Recognizing that we could lose a whole crop in the late summer hurricane season makes me want to build a hot box so we can get a quicker start on our first crop. That way, we can harvest our first crop in early May or so, and plant the second one.

And (also hopefully), if a hurricane starts barreling down on Florida or Mississippi late in the hurricane season, the second crop will be far enough along to be harvested.

In the end, it boils down to a personal choice. The next chapter will include instructions for how to build a hot box, if you decide to do so.

Whether you do, or not, you must do this:

You must sit down with your family, and decide which crops you want to raise. Bear in mind that watery vegetables, like tomatoes and watermelons, require much more water. That might not be an issue for you if there's a water source nearby like a playa lake or river.

Or, if you live in a dry area, and you plant watery vegetables like tomatoes and melons, you might conceivably be in a position of making a hard decision one day, when you're low on water. Do you give the plants most of the water and pray for rain? Or do you drink it and pray that your plants survive?

That would be a really tough choice to make.

Anyway, after you decide which vegetables and fruits you want to grow in the years ahead, hit the store and buy them.

I'd recommend you figure out the one person in your group who's got a green thumb, and put them totally in charge of agriculture. I would kill every plant we had, because I'm a plant killer. I don't mean to be, but I just am.

Once you select your resident gardener, have *her* (because green thumbs are usually attached to female hands) buy seeds that grow best in your area. Have her read the packages. For example, there may be twenty varieties of squash, but only a few that grow well in your climate.

Once she buys the seeds, have her seal them in an air tight container and set them on a shelf. But not in the garage, it can get too hot in there and damage the seeds.

Every springtime, when the new batch of seeds come out in the nurseries, have her replace the old ones. They're cheap, after all, and it'll pay going into the apocalypse with the freshest seeds possible.

Lastly, buy several large trash cans. The fifty gallon Hefty suckers with the snap on lids. The more of those you have, the more rain water you can capture and store while you're hunkered down. You'll use a lot of it for drinking water, of course. But you'll also need water for your crops. So... the more you can buy and keep, the better

And be sure to get ones with air tight lids.

That's so you can leave them full after each rainstorm stops (unless it's late in the season). The lids will keep the water from evaporating, and your gardener can use that water for her crops. Then she won't have to waste the water you boiled and made safe to drink.

33.
Building Your Hot Box

Okay, you'll be amazed at how simple this is to build. And you can do it for a hundred and ten bucks.

First, get your supplies. You'll need four fence posts that are ten feet long. Don't get the short ones, or your corn won't have room to grow. Make sure they are the ten foot size. I just priced them at Home Depot, and they're eleven bucks apiece.

Next, you'll nine two by four studs. Another eighteen bucks.

You'll need a sheet of half inch plywood. Get the cheap one for sixteen dollars.

Six bags of Sacrete: fourteen dollars.

A roll of heavy, 3.5 mil plastic sheeting (the clear kind, not black). $9.98.

Okay, that's $104. If you have a couple of dozen four inch screws or nails in your workshop you can use them. Otherwise, come by my house. I've got a boatload of them.

Or, you can buy a small box. That'll still keep you in budget...

1. Find the place in your yard that gets the most sun, without getting in the way of your rain catching activities. Like, for example, nowhere near the fence where you'll be hanging your rain tarp. Also, don't put it close to trees that will shade it. You want it to get as much sun as possible.

2. Once you decide where to put it, dig a hole. The hole needs to be eight feet long and four feet

wide. The exact size of the sheet of plywood. It also needs to be one foot deep. Just throw all the dirt into a big pile for now.

3. Place the sheet of plywood into the hole. The plywood will do several things. It will help act as a barrier from the cold ground below so your roots will be warmer in early spring. It will inhibit grass growth, and it will help retain water that would otherwise seep down into the water table.

4. Don't put the dirt back yet. Before you do that, take those post hole diggers you very seldom use out of your garage, or borrow them from your neighbor. On each corner of the *long* side of the plywood, dig a hole that's two feet deep. That's a foot deeper than your plywood hole. Dig these holes before you put the dirt back so you can still see the plywood. Otherwise, you might hit the plywood while you're digging the post holes.

5. Once you get the four holes dug, place the fence posts in them. Brace your fence posts so that they're standing upright. Use a tape measure to make sure they're all eight feet high, and modify the depth of your holes if you need to.

6. Use the secrete to fill in the holes around the posts. Just pour it dry. Once you're confident that the posts are straight and braced so they don't decide to lean, and the secrete is in place, pour water over the secrete to the top of the hole. Give it a minute to soak into the secrete, then fill the hole with water again.

* A quick note here: I know the instructions on the sack of Sacrete tell you to pour it into a tub, mix it with a specific amount of water, and stir well. Yada yada yada... You can go through all of that if you want. But I never do. I've been in the fencing business for almost thirteen years now, and I haven't had a post fall over yet. Just sayin'.

7. Use the dirt to cover up your plywood. While you're doing so, remove as much of the grass and roots as you can. The more you get out of the loose dirt now, the easier your gardener will have. She'll have to remove whatever you miss later, and it's much easier when the dirt is loose.

8. Let the concrete set for a couple of days.

9. Starting on the long sides, brace the posts with a two by four across the top, and a two by four across the middle.

10. Now go to the back side. Run two by fours across the top and the middle, and then trim off the excess.

11. Go to the front of the structure. This will be your entrance and exit. Run two by fours across the top and *bottom* and cut off the excess. (I know, you'll have a step to walk over every time you enter and leave the hot box, but you're supposed to. It's designed that way)

12. Run your last two by four from the center of the top of the doorway, across the structure to the center of the back of the structure (short side to short side).

13. The skeleton is finished. Wasn't that easy? Now you can make a choice. If you just want to leave the structure is, you may do so. Just put the roll of plastic in the garage until doomsday comes.

However, if you want to make use of it now, or try it out, here are the rest of the steps:

14. Start at the post to the left of the doorway. Your roll of plastic is twelve feet wide, and your post is only eight feet high. That's okay, because you want plenty of slack.

15. Staple or thumbtack the plastic to the top two by four on the long (left side) of your structure. Unroll the plastic as you go completely around it. Tack or staple it to the top two by fours as you go.

16. After you go completely around it, don't stop. Go an extra two feet, so that the plastic actually overlaps a bit. That'll help keep the sun's heat inside.

17. Throw some of the extra dirt from the post holes onto the excess plastic at the bottom of the structure. That'll keep the critters out and the heat in.

18. Take a roll of duct tape and go completely around the top of the structure, covering up the tacks or staples that were holding the plastic in place. Go around three so the plastic is good and secure.

19. Now take another piece of plastic and drape it over the open top. Make sure it drapes a foot on all four sides. That's your cap. Run duct tape all the way around your cap to hold it into place.

The key to keeping your plants warm is to keep this structure closed as much as possible in cold weather. Only go in it when you need to care for the plants, and pull the plastic "door" tightly against the structure when you enter or leave.

In the summer, heat can build up quickly in the hot box and it can get too hot in there on a very hot day. To keep your plants from drying out, simply open the door and put a rock on the plastic to keep it open. Or take the cap off of the top until the weather starts getting cool again..

3.5 mil plastic is pretty thick and durable. This structure will last you for at least a couple of years. As it starts to wear, though, you can extend its life by patching worn places with new plastic, or by taping a rip with duct tape.

34.
Dutch Ovens And Hard Tack

Most of you who have done a lot of camping know what a Dutch oven is. By camping, I don't mean living in an RV and watching a color television while everything that is beautiful about mother nature passes you by outside.

No, I'm talking about real camping. Living in a tent or sleeping under the stars. Catching your food or going hungry. Cooking the food over an open campfire.

Real camping.

Anyway, if you've ever done that, you've probably used a Dutch oven, or at least know what it is.

It's a specially designed skillet, normally made of cast iron, that sits on charcoal or over an open fire. The lid has a wide lip, so you can cook something else above the main dish. A secondary lid covers the food on top of the skillet, and in turn has another lid of its own. Frequently, the second lid has a lip on it and is flat so that you can put embers or charcoals on top to help do the cooking.

Over the years I've become a big fan of Dutch ovens. With a Dutch oven, you can fry bacon, then eggs in the main body of the oven, while biscuits are baking above it. Or, my favorite, catfish and biscuits.

My mom used to take flour and a few other ingredients, pick wild apples from a couple of trees along the Red River, and make homemade apple pie. While other families were roasting wieners and marshmallows, we were eating like royalty.

Or, depending on the kill of the day, you can make a variety of stews in a Dutch oven.

I only mention it because I'm a big fan of Dutch ovens (obviously, and because it's a viable alternative to the camp oven we talked about before). Like I said, they are generally cast iron, so they're durable. Even the stainless steel versions are pretty sturdy, so you can get years of use out of them.

They're also very flexible.

If, during a crisis, you still have electrical power or natural gas, you can use the bottom part on your stove as a regular skillet. You can use the top part as a baking dish, or a pie pan, or a flatbread pan.

But if you have no power, and you have no gas, you can still cook your food. And by cooking your entire meal at the same time, you'll save firewood or charcoal.

These things are normally a bit cheaper than the afore-mentioned camp oven. But if you can afford both, I'd recommend the investment. You'll thank yourself a thousand times when the day comes that you have to use them.

If you can't afford both of them, I'd recommend one or the other.

Okay. 'Nuff said about Dutch ovens.

Let's talk about hard tack. Which was the whole reason I brought up the Dutch oven to begin with.

For those of you who have never had it, it's like this. If a biscuit and a cracker got together and partied all night and got drunk and sloppy and bumped uglies, their resulting baby would be hardtack.

It would be an ugly little guy, hard as a rock and dry as a bone. It would taste like a cracker, but would be so thick and hard, it would be tough to chew.

That's the best way I can describe hard tack.

The first time I ever had hard tack was when my mom made it one camping trip when I was seven or eight. She said the recipe was passed down from her own mom, who survived the great depression. My grandmother had seven children, and my mom was the only girl. So you can imagine how hard it was to feed that family when the depression hit and there was no money to buy groceries.

Mom said they survived by eating nothing but hard tack and chicken grease for several months. And river water they boiled.

She made it on that hunting trip just to show us what it was like. She didn't eat any herself. I suppose she'd had enough of it when she was a girl. And I guess she wanted us to realize how good we had it.

The odd thing was, I didn't think it was really that bad. And I told Mom so.

She told me to eat it morning, noon and night for six months and see if I still liked it then.

If you Google "hard tack recipe," there are a dozen different recipes for making it.

I'd suggest two things…

You try several different recipes. Some are better than others. Sarah even modified one recipe and added grape jelly. It's still not going to win any

Betty Crocker awards, but the sweet grape taste made it a lot more tolerable.

The second thing I'd suggest is this. Once you find a recipe or two that you like, you make a lot of hard tack. Here's why:

The stuff lasts forever. As long as you keep it dry, like in an airtight container, it'll probably outlive you. That's because there isn't any moisture in it that would enable it to spoil.

The ingredients are cheap and easy. Basically flour, water, sugar and salt (and grape jelly if your name is Sarah Bennett). And, even if you're a single guy or your wife doesn't bake, the recipes are so simple that they're impossible to screw up.

Trust me. I even made a batch of them, and I can't boil water.

Here's the kicker. Even if you don't like hard tack, and even if you have no desire to ever eat them, they're still nice to have. If you don't eat them yourself, you can barter them to somebody else. Because when doomsday comes, you know darn well that there will be people out there who have been scavenging for food, and have been eating trash from dumpsters. Or playing Russian roulette with plants, trying to figure out which ones are poisonous and which ones are edible.

They'd love to have some hard tack. And people like that have been around, searching for food. And chances are if there's something you need, they'll know where to find it.

And then the hard tack that you don't particularly like and may never eat will come in very handy.

∎∎∎

Sarah Bennett's Hard Tack Recipe

Ingredients:
1 pound flour
½ pint water
½ tablespoon salt
¾ cup grape jelly (not preserves)

Mix all ingredients in a large mixing bowl until everything is thoroughly mixed. Make sure none of the powdered flour is still on the bottom of the bowl.

Roll the dough out until it's a quarter inch thick.

Use a cookie cutter or drinking glass to cut it into rounds about 3 inches across.

Place on a cookie sheet. Use a fork to poke holes throughout each piece so air in the batter can escape during baking.

Bake at 325 degrees Fahrenheit until they're a golden brown. Check at 35 minutes. If they're not crispy and dried out by then, bake them a few more minutes.

NOTE: This part is essential. You don't want them to burn, but you must bake out all of the moisture. Otherwise the batch will spoil

After the biscuits cool, wrap them in an airtight container. As long as air cannot get to them, they will last indefinitely.

These can be eaten on their own, or softened and served with a meal. They aren't bad when topped with brown or cream gravy, and set aside for several minutes to soften. Each biscuit is seventy calories.

■■■ ı

35.
Bartering For Keeps

I mentioned in an earlier chapter that making your own trail mix and storing it with your dry goods was an excellent idea for several reasons. First of all, it's easy to make and not that expensive if you make it yourself.

Secondly, it'll last for a very long time as long as you keep it dry.

Third, it's very high in calories, and if you get so low on food it'll keep your people alive.

And last, if you don't want or need it yourself, it makes great material to barter for ammunition, medicine, or something else you need.

When we discussed this before, I mentioned that there was a second great bartering item that you probably never thought of. And I promised to reveal it later.

Well, now's the time. The second thing that will be excellent bartering material is…

Toilet paper.

Stop laughing. I'm serious. On my Prepper's blog a couple of years ago I asked my followers to list the top ten things they didn't want to run out of if they were hunkered down in a survival situation.

The results, in order, were:
1. **Water**
2. **Food**
3. **Ammunition**
4. **Gasoline**
5. **Medicine**
6. **Toilet Paper**
7. **Antibiotics**

8. Firewood
9. Batteries
10. Transportation

The mere fact that it ranked higher than antibiotics or firewood indicated we put a pretty high value on this particular item.

It just so happened that the same week I took this survey, we got our income tax refund.

I think I already mentioned that we use our tax refund each year on prepping supplies. Our logic is that we were getting by without this money before we got it, so we can continue to get by without it if we spend it on our future survival needs.

Anyway, since the refund came in at the same time as the survey, we decided to spend a big chunk of the money on toilet paper.

Now, there are two ways you can buy a boatload of toilet paper.

You can go to Walmart or Sam's Club several times, buy a cart full of toilet paper, and notice on the third or fourth trip that people are starting to look at you funny.

Or, you can bear in mind that Amazon.com sells everything except nuclear bombs and gorilla snot. And for all I know, they may sell those too. I've never asked.

And if you sign up for Amazon Prime, they'll give you free shipping on most of the things you buy.

So Sarah ordered twenty cases of toilet paper. Each case contains 48 rolls.

I thought that was kind of excessive, until she explained.

She said she did the math and that ten people holed up for three years will use at least half of it. And we're likely to barter away some more of it. Lastly, once doomsday is over, depending on which of many scenarios happen, there's a good chance that manufacturing has taken a serious hit.

Or the trains and trucking system.

And there's a good chance that toilet paper will continue to be in short supply for a very long time.

So, she convinced me. And it helped to know that toilet paper will never go bad or wear out. So even if doomsday doesn't happen in our lifetimes (knock on wood), it won't go to waste.

And if that's the case, we may never have to buy toilet paper again.

That led me to my next dumb question, which was "Where in *hell* are we going to put twenty cases of toilet paper?"

Turns out she had an answer for that too.

What we did was sit down to play "Let's Make a Deal" with our teenage son. In exchange for him covering one whole wall in his bedroom, from floor to ceiling, with boxes, we'd let him take some spray paint and graffiti it up as much as he wanted.

He made a counter offer. He'd take the boxes off our hands, if we let him hang posters on them.

We said okay, and he hung fourteen posters of Selena Gomez and Taylor Swift on the boxes. Three were identical posters of Selena in a bikini. Apparently he liked that one particularly.

Ordinarily Sarah wouldn't have approved of his choice of posters, but surprisingly she didn't have a problem with them.

We've been worried for awhile, you see, that Zach spent too much time in his room and not enough time outside playing ball and stuff.

Sarah explained her logic this way:

"Well, at least his right arm will get plenty of exercise, even if the rest of his body doesn't."

Bartering itself will be a dangerous proposition in a world torn apart by crisis. You'll have to leave your compound and deal with people you may not know, and you may not know how desperate they are to get whatever you have to trade.

And even if you know them, they may have changed in the weeks or months when they were forced to live under miserable conditions.

My best advice is to make do the best you can, and only barter if you absolutely have to.

If you do have to barter, though, between the toilet paper and the trail mix you'll be in a great position to do so.

36.
Potatoes

I don't know if you like potatoes or not, but if you don't you really should start trying new ways to prepare them. That's because potatoes have the potential to be one of the three food staples in the years after doomsday ends.

The other two are corn and wheat. And depending on where you live, potatoes may grow better than the other two.

Potatoes require a bit more planning than other crops, because you can't just go to your local Walmart and buy a package of seeds.

You have to section an existing potato into pieces, each one having an "eye."

A plant will grow from the "eye," using the nutrients in the piece of potato to get it started, and until its roots start gathering nutrients and water on their own.

Here's the dilemma: say you're hunkered down in your residential fortress for three years. How do you make potatoes last that long without turning to mush?

The answer is simple. Well, maybe not. Actually the answer *is* simple, but the solution is a bit more complicated.

Remember when we talked about growing a couple of each vegetable every growing season, not necessary to eat, but rather to upgrade your seed supply?

Well, you'll do that with potatoes too. Only instead of planting seeds, you'll plant potato pieces.

You'll grow a few potatoes, and then you'll protect them until the next growing season. Then you'll repeat the process.

Once doomsday is over and you can grow crops out in the open without fear of someone taking them, you can take those few potatoes and use the entire output to plant a much bigger crop. By the second year after breakout, you'll be able to grow enough potatoes to feed a significant number of people.

There are a couple of problems you'll have to contend with. First of all, raw potatoes won't normally survive a long winter season. Secondly, they grow much better in very loose soil. The hard-compacted soil in your back yard won't be very compatible.

We've been kicking this problem around for two years now, and here's what we're doing:

1. We always keep a five pound bag of potatoes on the bottom shelf in the pantry. It's cool and dark in there, and potatoes like cool and dark. They'll keep much longer.

2. Sarah checks on them every few days. When they begin to bud, she'll replace them with another bag. And she'll slice up the old ones, dry them out in the oven, and add them to our dry stock.

3. When the apocalypse happens, and we're stuck in the house for a long period of time, she will take the potatoes and place each one in an individual zip lock sandwich bag. Normally we're

big fans of generic products, but we're going with Glad on this one.

4. Potatoes will last much longer in an airless environment. So she will take each potato and place it in its own bag. Then she'll zip the bag closed *almost* all the way. All the way until she gets to a straw that she'll place in the corner of the bag.

5. That's right. She'll use the straw to suck as much air as possible out of the bag before she pulls out the straw and seals it.

6. The first time I saw her do this I made an unwise comment about her sucking ability. She threw a potato at me.

7. Anyway, all plastic bags leak air eventually. So she'll take the bagged potatoes and put them into a second zip-lock bag, and suck the extra air out of it as well.

8. Then she'll take the potatoes and put them into a plastic tub. She'll pack the tub around them with potting soil. This is the same potting soil she will plant the potatoes in when spring comes around.

And here's the thing with potting soil. For some reason it has excellent insulation qualities. Don't ask me how or why. It just does.

9. She'll put the snap-on lid onto the plastic tub full of potatoes and potting soil and will place it in the center of our safe room.

10. Our safe room, you might recall, will be the place where anyone who isn't sleeping or on sentry duty will spend most of the time. It's the room we'll run power to from our generator. It'll have a light for reading, and for two or three hours a day we'll be able to watch DVDs. We'll even have a microwave, so we can heat up cups of instant hot cocoa or coffee when the generator is running. I'm guessing that last item will be pretty popular in the dead of winter.

11. Now, the TV and DVD player will only be on occasionally. So will the light. But on top of the tub full of potatoes that Sarah has turned into a coffee table will sit three candles that will burn twenty four hours a day.

12. Now, three candles won't heat this room all by itself. After all, it's not air tight. It can't be, with candles burning in the room. But the doorway will have a shower curtain rod stretched across it. Instead a door, a shower curtain will be opened and closed to keep as much heat in as possible. And when we go in or out of the safe room, we'll have to duck down. That's because the doorway will only be five feet high.

That's because heat rises, you see. And while the room will never be toasty, what heat that is generated by the three candles and the body heat from several people constantly being in there will rise. The warmest part of the room will be between the top of the doorway and the ceiling. About head high.

13. In theory, this room will never drop below freezing. Between the candles, the body heat, and the fact that the room will have no windows, we think we can pretty much ensure that.

14. And the potatoes will survive, as long as they don't freeze. Even if the temperature gets close to freezing, they'll still have the insulation provided by the potting soil to help them make it through.

15. In the spring, Sarah will remove the potatoes from their zip lock bags and plant them into the same tub the spent the winter in, and another tub just like it.

16. Potatoes like loose soil. In hard pack soil it takes them longer to grow, because they have to push the hard soil out of the way. In loose soil, though, it's much less work for them. They tend to grow larger and faster.

17. She could dig out a place in the yard to plant them, and replace the soil with the potting soil. But it's lighter than regular soil and the rains would eventually wash it away. Plus, the tubs will allow her to bring the plants back inside if we should have a late freeze.

18. By planting the potatoes in the early spring, she'll be able to grow two crops. And although she'll only have space in the tubs to grow a few potatoes, she'll get enough from the second harvest to get to the next planting the following year

19. As I stated before, I've killed every plant I've ever tried to grow. I don't know beans about gardening. But Sarah does, and so does Cinda. So this is one case when I'm just going to sit back, shut up, and trust them.

37.
The Pet Dilemma

Let me warn you going in that this is going to be a very sensitive subject.

If your family is like most, your pets are more than just animals. They're more like a part of the family. And we can't bear to do without them.

By the way, when I say "pets," I'm talking about dogs. I can't think of a single good reason to keep a cat around in a doomsday situation.

But hey, I don't like cats. Plus, I'm allergic to the little bastards. And although I can't understand why, I know that some people like them. So keep them if you will.

And let's face it. Dogs can be darn useful in a prepping situation. They can sense a prowler and alert us, even if we're unable to see him. They're also very effective at scaring prowlers away.

But when your family is holed up in a house that's supposed to be vacant, a barking dog is a liability. Anyone with any sense knows that if there's a dog in the back yard, there are people in the house who take care of it.

And even worse, they'll know that the people in the house have so much food and water that they can afford to share it with the dog.

And that's a *major* problem.

What I'm hinting at is that you may ultimately have to make a decision on whether or not to shoot your dogs to prevent them from giving you away.

And I'm not necessarily advocating that you do so. You may determine, based on your own situation, that the dogs are more an asset than a liability. Like I said, they do make great early warning systems, and will protect you to their dying breath.

But the best option is not to put you in a position of having to make that decision.

Consider this:

About the time Sarah and I decided to get really serious about prepping, our cat Toby got out of the yard and was hit by a car in front of our house.

And before you accuse me of throwing the cat under the passing car, I am completely innocent. I don't like cats, but this was our family pet. Everyone in the family was quite fond of Toby except me.

Anyway, we had the opportunity to get another cat, but I was able to talk Sarah out of it. I gave her my big puppy dog eyes and reminded her that it's so much easier for me to breathe at night when there's no cat around.

She agreed that breathing is a very good thing. But she still wasn't convinced.

Then I told her that hey, maybe a cat wasn't such a bad idea after all. I told her that since we were convinced that doomsday was coming, it wouldn't hurt to have an extra ten pounds of protein readily available, and that it would make a tasty meal if we ran out of food.

She decided that another cat wasn't a good idea.

Around that same time, we noticed that the whiskers on our black lab, Sparky, were getting very very gray.

Hannah asked for a puppy for Christmas that year. She tried her damnest to talk us into getting her one.

She said, "It'll be great! We can get another black lab like Sparky, and he can encourage Sparky to get more exercise and move around a little more. They can be best friends."

One of the hardest things I ever had to do was tell Hannah the reason why we wouldn't let her have a new puppy.

We sat on the couch together, and I held her hand, and told her that if we got her the puppy, we might have to shoot it someday when the world became a very ugly place. And I asked her if she could put herself through that.

She cried, but just a bit. And here's the thing. She understood, and agreed. That's when I realized that my baby is growing up faster than I ever imagined.

She did ask me a question, though, that troubled me. She asked, "What if it happens while Sparky is still alive? Can you pull the trigger on Sparky?"

It was a sad thought. Sparky had been with us for thirteen years.

Luckily, I never had to make that decision. Sparky died last summer. He went peacefully in his sleep. I buried him next to my pecan tree, so he'll always be in the shade.

So, now all we've got left are two aquariums full of fish. And nobody feels any particular affection for them.

I guess what I'm saying is this. Every situation is different. You know your neighborhood better than I do. You know your back yard better than I do. You know your pets better than I do.

It may be that you can keep a dog in your yard that isn't visible to looters or marauders walking down your street.

It may be possible that you can train your dog to be quiet when strangers are around, instead of barking his head off.

And it may be possible that you decide, based on your own situation, that having a dog for added protection is worth the additional risk.

All I'm suggesting is an alternative. Something to think about.

Perhaps the best way to avoid having to make that really difficult decision someday is to stop getting new pets until the apocalypse is over.

38
A Different Kind of Dilemma

I have a casual friend who's also a prepper. We belong to the same VFW hall. I don't know him that well, but he seems like a nice enough guy and since we're both preppers we occasionally compare notes.

We also belong go to the same range and I see him there occasionally. It was at the range a couple of weeks ago that he mentioned he had some "treated" ammunition he planned to use when doomsday hit.

I asked him what he meant and he explained that he took three boxes of bullets and dipped the tips in his own excrement. He said that if he didn't get a kill shot, the next best thing was for his target to get a dreadful infection and die a slow and miserable death.

I thought he was kidding. I thought he was going to go through this long explanation of how he dipped the bullets in excrement just so he could come up with some stupid punch line, like, "and that's where the term 'dipshit' came from."

But he was dead serious.

I honestly didn't know what to say, so I stumbled around for some words and wound up asking him, "Doesn't that throw off the balance of the bullet and screw up your shot? And doesn't it foul your weapon?

His answer to both questions was "no."

He said he was careful to only leave a "light coating" on the bullets and to remove any visible particles with a Q-Tip. And he said he took two boxes of the treated bullets to the range and did comparison fires, and it seemed to have no affect on his scores.

And it made me think. Now, I was a United States Marine for almost half my life. I've fired most of the small arms in the Marine Corps arsenal, and made marksman on the M-16, M-9 and .38 (yes, I'm that old). I can still make a head shot at a hundred yards nineteen times out of twenty. With a handgun, at 25 yards, I'm just as consistent.

But my friend, he's a different story. I know, because I've seen him shoot at the range. At a hundred yards, his head shots are more often than not going to take off an ear, or miss completely. His center mass torso shots are just as likely to hit a shoulder as the heart.

He has a real problem with his breathing and trigger control, and he's kind of a nervous and twitchy kind of guy by nature.

I've given him pointers a couple of times, and so has one of the instructors who hangs out there. But you can only help some people so much. He'll appear to be listening, and make a couple of good shots, and we'll pat him on the back and say "good job."

And then he'll go back to his old bad habits and start missing his target again.

If you spend any time at shooting ranges, you probably know the type.

Anyway, I have been struggling with this one for awhile, and I think I can see where he's coming from. I mean, if someone tries to kill you once, and you can't be sure of taking him out, do you want to give him another chance to come back and try again?

Or is putting shit on the end of your bullets just too far out there, too sadistic, a tactic to use?

I mentioned this in my blog last week and asked for feedback. The responses I got were about fifty-fifty. Half of the guys said that if anybody tried to kill them, they deserved what they got, to include a serious infection that would either kill them or keep them laid up for awhile.

The other half said it was inhumane, and that my friend needed to learn how to shoot better.

I asked Sarah the same question. At first she was disgusted by the whole idea. Then she gave it some serious thought.

She finally said, "I know you're not comfortable with this, Charlie. But even you miss a shot occasionally. And if there were somebody out there who was trying to kill us, would you want them to come back for a second attempt at you, at me, at our children?"

I'm still struggling with this one. In the end, it's as much a question of survival as it is a moral dilemma. I guess it's up to each man's conscience.

39.
Making Full Use of Your Resources

This next bit of advice may sound a bit strange on the face of it, but it'll make perfect sense once I explain.

My wife and I take the kids out to dinner every Friday night, unless one of the boys has a football game. Then we go out on Saturday night instead.

I only mention that because that's the one occasion each week when Sarah and I can count on being in the same car at the same time.

So we also use the opportunity to do something else.

Before we head out to the restaurant, we always cruise up to the end of our street, and then down the two streets next to ours.

What we're looking for are houses that are for sale, or vacant, or recently foreclosed.

It may sound like an odd habit, but we want to stay current on where the other vacant houses are close by. And here's why:

When the apocalypse strikes, in whatever form it may take, we need to have an evacuation site should we ever come under heavy fire.

We also need to have a safe place nearby where we can stash some extra supplies in case something else happens to our house and have to bug out temporarily.

And lastly, we need to know where we can go to safely gather firewood and insulation.

Vacant houses provide all three.

Ideally, you'll have a vacant house that's close enough to you to allow you to move back and forth unseen. And if not unseen, at least unchallenged.

I've lived in suburbs that have alleyways which run behind each row of houses. The main purpose of the alleys is for trash collection. Some cities put dumpsters in the alleys for household trash. The alleys also give utility companies easy access to high wires and meters and other cool stuff.

If you're lucky enough to have such an alley behind your house, it can be used to access a vacant house on the street next to yours. But you'll have to know the vacant house is there.

Our housing development doesn't have alleys. We put our garbage cans out by the street. In a doomsday scenario, that can be a good thing and a bad thing. It's bad because it doesn't provide an alley to give us easy access to other vacant houses in the area. But it's good because that same alley would give marauders more access to us.

Since we don't have an alley, we share a back fence with a huge two story house directly behind us.

We're quite familiar with the house behind us, and know its history.

Three years ago the man that lived there came home early from a business trip and found his wife in bed with another man. Bad for him. He shot and killed them both, presumably mid-stroke. Bad for them.

And it was equally bad for the house. It was temporarily seized by the state until after his murder trial for evidentiary purposes. So it was vacant for a year.

To try to recoup some of the money they'd lost on the deal, Wells Fargo sold the house in a hurry, to a family who had no business buying it. They were in way over their heads. It was much more than they could afford, and way more house than they needed.

Everyone in the neighborhood knew it was just a matter of time.

And sure enough, in just over a year they were hopelessly behind on their mortgage payments and unable to work out a deal with the bank. So they were served with foreclosure paperwork.

This couple didn't go out quietly, though. They somehow blamed the bank for their financial problems, maybe because everybody else in the country was blaming the banks at that time.

And they decided they wanted to send a message to the bank. So before they left they bought a dozen rats from a local pet store and infested the attic. They made a point to kick a hole in every single wall in every single room, ripped all the light fixtures from the ceilings and shattered the toilets and sinks.

Then as a final shot, they turned on the faucet for the upstairs bath tub and left the house for the last time, twisting the key off in the doorknob on their way out.

The bank claimed they did $70,000 in damages to a house that was only appraised at $130,000.

The house has understandably been vacant since then. The bank has sued the homeowner to recoup their money, and I say good luck with that. They'll never get a dime.

It's listed on the federal foreclosure website for $72,500. I'm not sure how the law works, but someone told me that when you buy a foreclosed home you have to make repairs before you can actually move into it.

If that's true, then somebody's going to have to pay seventy grand up front to buy a house that had two murders committed in it and was infected with rats.

Not likely to be a strong selling point when there are other decently priced houses in the neighborhood without such baggage.

Bad for the bank. Good for us.

Because we expect the house to be vacant for the foreseeable future.

And if it's still vacant when doomsday hits, we have big plans for it.

As I said, we share a back fence with the property. If doomsday hits, I plan to make a hidden gate in the center of that fence. I already have six slide bolts in my garage for that very purpose.

If doomsday hits and the house is still vacant, it will become our evacuation point. We will store several days worth of no-cook food and water there, in metal rat-proof boxes, hidden inside the walls that were conveniently kicked in for us. We'll also store an extra rifle and handgun, and enough ammunition to allow us to take back our own house when the time is right. There will be blankets and pillows, in case we're there for a couple of days.

One of the most frustrating things about prepping is that although we can all foresee bad things on the horizon, we don't know what form it will take, or how long it will last.

If it's just rioting and civil unrest, or a collapse of the economy, it might only last a few months before the military quells the riots or Congress gets its shit together (yeah, right) and stabilizes the economy enough to start functioning again.

On the other hand, if it's a dirty bomb attack (or a real nuclear attack) by terrorists, a major electromagnetic storm or a meteorite that sends a dust cloud into the atmosphere, it could last for months or years.

We are stocking plenty of propane and charcoal to heat our food and purify our water. But if doomsday lasts longer than our fuel supply, we have to have a Plan B.

Our Plan B is the same house we'll use for evacuation purposes, whether it's the one behind us or another one close by.

And our Plan B is simple. If we run out of propane and charcoal before doomsday is over, we will very methodically dismantle the house and use whatever we can.

I'm not just talking firewood, either. Although that's the main thing we'd get from it, we can gather carpet padding to help insulate our own house from icy winter temperatures. The bathtubs will be dragged into the back yard, and we'll fasten two by fours onto the roof to direct rainwater into them. Even the carpet fibers can be used as kindling to get fires going.

The main thing, though, will be the two by fours and two by sixes.

The average person doesn't realize how much wood is in a house. Yes, it's a pain to get out, and can be dangerous if not done carefully. And I'm not an expert by any means. But I'll bet a steak dinner that there's enough wood in an average two story to keep a small campfire burning nonstop for a year. And for a periodic campfire, one that's burned only for a few hours a night on moonless nights, it would last a lot longer than that.

Tim and I put our heads together and figured out exactly how we plan to do it.

And, like I said, I'm no expert. You can probably devise your own plan that's just as effective. But here's how we plan to gather our wood while remaining stealthy (no chain saws) and reasonably safe.

We'll start in the attic. We'll go up at night, with flashlights, after covering the ventilation windows so that out light doesn't shine through.

Then we'll use old fashioned hand saws to cut long pieces of wood and drop them onto the second floor below.

Not all of them, of course. We'll take out every second or third piece. And we'll keep a close eye on the roof. When it starts to sag, or starts to creak and moan, we'll move out of the attic to the second floor.

As I said, the former owners of the house behind us kicked holes in every single wall. They didn't know it, but they started our work for us. We'll finish kicking out the sheetrock, and use crow bars to pry out every third stud.

Eventually, of course, it'll get too hairy to continue. On the second floor.

Instead of working to remove studs out of the first floor walls, we will remove the siding from the back side of the house. It's wood planking, so all by itself it'll give us plenty of wood to burn.

Once the siding is off, the plywood exterior will be exposed. We'll pry it off with crowbars and break it into burnable sized pieces.

Then we'll be looking at the two by four studs on the exterior wall of the back of the house.

Our plan is to collapse the house. But to do it as safely as possible. So what we're going to do is go inside the house, and hammer a nail into each two by four, about six inches off the floor.

Once that's done, we'll take a keyhole saw and make a cut on each two by four, from the outside of the building, about three quarters of the way through, just below the nails.

Since we're only going three quarters of the way through, we don't anticipate any problems with the house falling before we're ready for it to. But we'll be ready to run if it does.

Once the nails are in place and the cuts are made, the rest is done by brute strength.

If you've ever cut down a tree, you'll know that your first cut, the notch, is always made in the direction you want the tree to fall. If you want the tree to fall to the west, you cut a big notch on the west side of the tree. Then you make a second cut on the east side and let the weight of the tree make it fall. In this case, since the notch is on the west side, it cannot fall to the east. It will look for the path of least resistance. That's something my high school physics teacher used to say, but I never quite understood it until I cut down my first tree.

Anyway, our collapsing the house will be sort of like cutting down a tree, in that we'll make cuts to the exterior wall's studs. Because of the cuts, the wood can only break in one direction: outward.

In the back of my garage, on the top shelf, is two hundred feet of rope. Good old fashioned hemp rope. We got hemp because the nylon rope is way too stretchy.

There's a lot of dust on the rope now, because since I bought it I've never had any use for it, and since we started having kids Sarah doesn't like to play those games where I tie her to the bed anymore (joking, sort of).

Anyway, in a survival situation I'm probably going to find other uses for rope, but the main reason it's on that dusty shelf in my garage is for partially collapsing a house.

We'll take the rope and cut it into pieces about twenty feet long. We'll take each section of rope and loop it around each two by four, resting on top of the nail, and just above the cut in the wood.

Then it's just a matter of putting two strong men on each side of the rope and playing something similar to tug-of-war. The plan is to pull each two by four outward until it snaps, and to keep doing that until the back part of the house collapses.

Anyway, this method sounds good in theory. I was in the military for a long time, and I know that things don't always go according to plan. If the house doesn't fall as easily as we're hoping, or if there are some other problems we didn't plan for, we'll take a step back, regroup, and try again. But we will never surrender. It's not the way of the Corps.

After the house is partially collapsed, it'll be a lot easier to deal with. Safer, too.

Then we'll literally be able to pick it to pieces. We can pick up crap we don't need, like shingles or sheetrock, and throw them into a discard pile. At the same time, things we can use, like lumber, plywood or particle board will be put to good use.

And after the initial demolition pile is finished, the rest of the house can theoretically be brought done a little at a time in the same manner.

Bear in mind that this wouldn't be done all at one time. It would happen over the course of several months, each time we went back to the house to gather firewood. And we'd prefer not to tear the house down at all.

It is, however, an option.

If you run out of wood and need more, we recommend you try this method. You may have to modify if depending on your particular situation. And it is critical that you know exactly which houses in your neighborhood are vacant when the event happens. Going into an occupied house that you think is vacant may get you shot.

40.
Growing Crops for the Long Term

There's another good reason to know where the vacant houses in your neighborhood are.

Besides providing emergency shelter and a source of firewood, they can also provide you more space to grow your crops.

With any luck, when doomsday happens it will be resolved within just a few weeks or months, and everyone can come out of their shelters and play nice with each other and start making the world livable again.

But since we don't know what form the disaster is going to take, or how long it's going to last, we cannot rely on that being the case.

In other words, we must hope for the best, but plan for the worst.

That's why we discussed the need to cultivate seeds in an earlier chapter. Because if the disaster, whatever it may be, drags on long enough, we will all eventually run out of food.

And that would be a problem.

That's where the whole seed thing comes in. We must assume that we'll run out of food before the world gets back to normal, and that we'll have to grow our own.

Trouble is, most people don't have enough room in their back yards to grow enough food to sustain everyone in their group.

Back to the vacant houses. At the same time you commandeer a vacant house to use as firewood, you can also commandeer the house's back yard to give you more growing space.

Every situation is different. Hopefully, you'll have a couple of vacant yards nearby you can use for this purpose.

In Book 2 of this series, we'll talk about setting up a block alliance, if you will, for the purpose of providing mutual protection for everyone on your street. We'll talk about how to cordon off your block on each end to make it inaccessible to vehicle traffic or outsiders, and how to remove all the trees from the front yards. Then we'll talk about how to use the front yards on your street to grow enough food for all of the block's residents.

But for now, we'll assume that your neighbors are all assholes who cannot be trusted. We'll assume you and your group are in this thing alone, and having to fend for yourself.

In that case, a typical back yard probably won't grow enough subsistence crops (corn, wheat or potatoes) to keep your group alive.

But two yards would.

Your situation will differ from mine, of course. But here are my plans if the house behind mine is still vacant when the disaster strikes.

I plan to remove the back fence that divides our two yards. I may not need it for firewood, but I'll put it aside in a pile in case I do. I will install screws along the top of the fence to fortify it like I've done the fence surrounding my own yard.

In fact, I already snuck over there one day not long ago with a cordless electric drill. I went around the yard and drilled two small holes at the top of each fence slat. I have two boxes of screws in the garage, and when doomsday comes I can put screws in all the holes in half a day or so.

Shhhh. Don't tell anybody I drilled holes in the bank's fence, okay?

Anyway, the reason I did that is because someday I may commandeer that yard. And then I'll start prepping it to grow crops.

Prepping it means cutting down the tree in the back yard. More firewood if we ever need it. Then digging up the grass.

Yes, I know it will take some time to get it ready to plant, but with no back fence to hinder us, we can prepare our own yard at the same time.

And remember that we'll have more time that we'll know what to do with. Any time any of us are bored, we can be like, "There's the shovel, go dig for a couple of hours."

One of the biggest problems you'll have to deal with if you're sheltered in place for any length of time is boredom. People in your group will go nuts, looking for things to do to kill time.

My guess is that you'll have people fighting over the shovel.

If you've never prepped your yard for a garden, you'll be surprised how simple it is.

In a nutshell, you simply turn over the soil, wait a couple of days until the grass dies, and then pull it out. Then do the same thing again. Some of the grass will be under the soil each time, so you'll have to repeat the process three or four times. Keep doing it until you're confident that you got all the grass roots. That'll make it a lot easier to keep the grass from coming back once you start planting crops there.

Of course, in a non-survival situation, you'd rent or borrow a tiller to do the digging for you.

In a survival situation, though, that's a bad idea, even if you happen to have your own tiller.

First of all, of course, is the noise. You don't want to advertise to everyone in the neighborhood that you're building a garden.

And trust me. They'd figure it out. What other purpose would you have for running a tiller?

Secondly is the boredom thing. It'll do your team good to work together on a common goal. It'll give them something to do to help pass their time, and it'll get them out of the house where they can get some fresh air and exercise. And when the crops start coming in, they'll share in a sense of accomplishment. Because everyone will have had a hand in making it happen.

The ideal situation, of course, would be for there to be a vacant house next door to you or directly behind you. If that's not the case, though, you can still use the back yard of the nearest vacant house. You'll have to be careful when you go back and forth to work it, and I'd strongly recommend you send an armed escort along with anyone going to work the plot.

I'd also suggest you post a warning sign that tells others you've claimed this land as your own, and that you will defend it if necessary.

That won't keep everybody away, but it'll scare away some of them.

Once you actually plant your crops, you'll have to post a guard twenty four hours a day. And he'll have to have a radio in case he needs to call for backup.

I know that'll throw a wrench into your security plans, but it's essential to keep people from digging up your plants and stealing them, or from harvesting your crop before you do.

And along those lines, here's another small thought.

Sometimes it's best to offer a peace pipe instead of a bullet.

What I mean by that is this… if you can afford to give a couple of your plants to your neighbors to start their own crops, or a handful of seeds, it can go a long way toward fostering good will and a sense of family in the neighborhood. And it might just keep you from getting shot late one night while you're watching over your corn.

If you do that, though, be sure you give the recipient of your generosity some specific instructions.

Tell them that you aren't giving them plants (or seeds) for eating. Tell them you're giving them the capability of making more seeds. And they are to take those two or three plants (or seeds) you give them and to grow them and garner more seeds. And that a year later they should have enough seeds to plant a substantial crop.

And tell them there won't be any more. If they take your two corn plants and grow them and then eat the corn instead of saving it, then they're stupid and out of luck.

Be sure they understand that.

Hopefully they will take your plant and grow their two corn stalks, and then use the twelve ears of corn to have enough seeds for three hundred plants the following year.

And hopefully they'll remember your generosity and become a good ally. Or at least, no longer a potential enemy.

And hopefully they'll do the same good deed for someone else, and eventually everyone in the neighborhood can grow their own food and leave yours the hell alone.

Even after you harvest your crops, it is critically important that you save enough seeds for the next year's crop. And never, ever plant all of your seeds. Always hold some back.

That's because if you plant all of your seeds and an early freeze, or tornado, or heavy rainstorm, or anything else kills your crop, you'll be able to try again. If you don't have any standby seeds, you're pretty much screwed.

I'll talk more about this in the sequel to this book, but eventually the world will get back to normal again. It will be important that you and your neighbors get together for mutual protection, and at that time you'll work together for a lot of things.

You'll take care of the old and sick, work together to provide security, and will start growing community crops. It just makes more sense to do it that way. By working together and sharing planting, weeding and watering duties, you can grow a much bigger crop that's capable of feeding everyone on your block.

But only if you have enough extra seeds to get started.

So always, always, save a good batch of seeds at harvest time.

Always.

41.
A Secret Gate

Just a little footnote related to the last chapter, and an idea that will come in handy during your non-planting endeavors as well...

If you do have another yard nearby you can use to grow crops, you'll need to have easy access to get to and from it. Whether you have an alley behind your house or not, you'll need an easy and quick way to get in and out of your own yard.

Again, I'm working on the assumption that you live in a suburb like most of us do, and that you have a wooden privacy fence like most of us do. If you don't live in a suburb, this won't apply to you at all. If you live in a suburb but don't have a wooden privacy fence, you may be able to modify this somewhat to meet your own situation.

If you do have a wooden privacy fence, try this solution:

1. If you have an alley behind your house, but it's for utility company access and not for trash collection, you probably don't have a gate. If that's the case, take a handsaw to your back fence. Place it between two of the slats. Then saw completely through the top brace that runs between the fence posts.

2. Take a slide bolt and install it across the cut you just made. This will work whether the two-by four is on the inside or the outside of your fence.

3. Move over six slats and do the same thing. Cut the wood, then install the slide bolt.

4. Now move down to the center and bottom braces and do the same thing. Be sure you install the slide bolts after each cut. Otherwise the fence will shift and they won't line up right.

When you're done, you'll have a secret gate that can be removed in ten seconds or less, and put back in place in twenty seconds or less. It'll allow you to slip out of your yard easily, day or night. You'll need someone to let you back in, but your rear sentry should see you coming and can send somebody out.

Note: you should never have to wait or call for someone to let you back into your yard. If you do, you may want to fire your sentry. He's been sleeping on the job.

This method works equally well if you don't have an alley behind your house. Of course, you probably have a gate from your back yard to the front, but if it's inaccessible for some reason, use this method on the other side of the house.

If you do have to exit through your front yard to get to your vacant house, try not to do it in the daytime any more than you have to.

Say, for example, you're sending two men across the street and two doors down to the nearest vacant house. One to work and the other to stand watch. Send them out before dawn. That way they only have to come out in the open once during daylight, on their way back.

Or better yet, have them pack food and water, take frequent breaks, switch off between digging and watching, and work until dusk. Hey, our grandfathers who were farmers worked from dawn to dusk. Your guys can too. You can reward them by giving them a couple of days off to sleep and recover.

Or, if you're doing okay on food, you can ask for volunteers for such a detail, and then reward them with an extra bag of trail mix or a candy bar or something.

You'd be surprised at how much a man will do for a Snickers bar when he hasn't had one for six months. Ask any Marine just back from Afghanistan what he missed the most. He'll tell you his kids, Snickers and sex, in that order.

Well, maybe not. But he will say his kids first.

42.
Some Odds and Ends

Okay, we left off talking about Snickers bars, which kinda brings us back to my favorite subject: food. That's good, because I want to mention a few more things before I wrap this up.

First off, I wasn't kidding about the Snickers bars. Or something similar. I know they're just empty calories, but I'm not talking about counting them in with your food stores.

I'm talking about bonus calories. To help you celebrate special occasions. Or to reward good behavior. Say you're running low on antibiotics. You ask for volunteers to go down to the old Walgreen's store to see if the looters left any behind. It's a dangerous mission, so you might sweeten the pot by offering a couple of Snickers bars to whoever's willing to do it.

On your kids' birthdays you can stick a candle into a Snicker's bar and sing "Happy birthday." It's not much, but it may be the best you can do.

And you can do it on a budget, too. Here's how.

Sarah has these weird storage things that slide under the bed in our bedroom. I don't know if they have a name, but they're made of plastic and have snap on lids, and they're only about four inches high. We have three of them, and they take up nearly all of the floor space under the bed.

Every year at Halloween, she pulls them out. They're full of candy from the previous year. Little candy bars of every flavor, suckers, Milk Duds, you name it. It's the candy she passes out to the trick-or-treaters.

Now, this candy is a year old. But the kids don't care. Nobody has ever once said, "Gee, Mr. Bennett, your little bag of Skittles didn't taste very fresh."

Nope. They don't care because they're kids. And kids will drop an ice cream bar into the dirt, and then pick it back up, brush off the dirt and eat it.

Kids don't care if candy is a year old when they eat it, and you won't either in a survival situation. Really.

The day after Halloween, Sarah hits Walmart and a couple of the grocery stores. She stocks up on candy, but gets it for half price or less. She refills the containers and slides them back under the bed. And yes, she throws in some full sized Snickers bars too.

And, whenever doomsday strikes, underneath our bed we'll have a good supply of treats that will occasionally brighten the day of people we care about for several years.

I mention the candy thing because if you follow Sarah's lead you'll have enough goodies to reward the people on your team and celebrate good times occasionally. And when the world is crashing down around us, it'll boost everybody's morale every once in awhile if they can have a Tootsie Roll Pop and feel normal again. Even if it's just for a few minutes.

Now, then. Let's talk about Meals, Ready to Eat. MREs. If you're a prepper, you already know what they are. You may even have some. And that's not necessarily a bad thing. They've come a long way since the first generation MREs I ate as a young recruit. I know because I had them periodically throughout my military days, and they got a little bit better every time I ate them.

And they last a very long time. Up to ten years, if they're stored right. They're chock full of calories, which is a good thing in a survival situation. And they come in enough different varieties so that you don't have to eat the same thing day after day.

Like I said, I've got nothing against MREs.

Well, maybe one thing… the price.

For crying out loud, a pickup full of MREs costs more than the price of the truck.

I think most of it is because some (not all, but some) of the manufacturers are taking advantage of us because they know there are a lot of us preppers out there. And they know that if you and I don't pay a premium price for their MREs, then somebody else will.

But I won't, and here's why:

In a survival situation, I can store four years worth of food for the same amount of money as two years worth of MREs.

Stated that way, it kind of makes sense, doesn't it?

I know a guy I used to work with. He's a prepper too, but he's not going to be part of my group. I've never compared paychecks with him, but I think we're pretty much on the same income level.

About a year ago he started stocking up on MREs. Every time he got a few extra bucks, he'd order some on line. UPS would drop them at his doorstep and he'd store them somewhere in his house.

I tried to convince him he could do better on his own and he scoffed.

So I said, "Do what you want to do. But if you only store enough MREs to survive for two years and doomsday lasts longer than that, don't come knocking on my door looking for food. Because I'll tell you that if you'd followed my advice in the first place you'd have four years worth of food. Then I'll shoot your stupid ass just for being a stupid ass."

Truth is, I more than likely won't really shoot him. But I damn sure won't give him any food, either.

We talked several chapters ago about canned ravioli and Vienna sausages and spaghetti sauce and stuff. It's okay to buy those things, as long as you keep an eye on the expiration dates and have a plan to rotate such items before they go out of date.

We also talked about all of the ways to dehydrate your own vegetables and meats for future use. You can do all that for a fraction of the cost of MREs.

Here's a couple of other ideas:

Spaghetti noodles are dirt cheap. Walmart gets $1.92 for a two pound box. And a two pound box may not sound like much, but consider this:

Take a three gallon stew pot and fill it with unfiltered rainwater. Boil it for ten minutes to purify it. Then add in two small jars of chicken bouillon powder, that two pound box of spaghetti noodles, a handful of dried chicken chunks, and a quarter cup of dried sliced celery. Let the concoction boil for another twenty minutes and then take it off the fire.

Put a lid on it and let it soak overnight.

The next day you'll have three gallons of chicken noodle soup.

It will look *exactly* like Campbell's chicken noodle soup. And it will taste *almost* exactly like it, too. I say almost exactly because I think the homemade version actually tastes better. But that's just me.

And guess what? You just fed ten people for a day. For less than six bucks.

How many MREs could you have bought for six bucks? One point three, maybe? That's one point three people you could have fed for the same amount of money.

I've got a boatload of boxed spaghetti noodles in our food stores. They come in plastic bags, too, but the boxes are easier to stack and to inventory. And whether or not they come in boxes or bags, they last pretty much forever.

So, when the shit hits the fan, we'll be eating a lot of spaghetti the first few months, to get rid of the canned pasta we have in the pantry. Once the canned pasta is gone, we'll still have a lot of spaghetti noodles we can prepare in other ways. Like the aforementioned chicken noodle soup. Sarah also likes to make spaghetti noodles mixed with cream of mushroom soup. That comes in a powder form, by the way, so it's shelf stable and will last as long as the noodles last. Same with spaghetti noodles and country gravy. Also in powder form.

Use your imagination. Experiment now, and get creative.

A lot of people turn up their nose at Ramen noodles. I happen to like them. They're cheap (you can't beat a meal for 14 cents) and not bad. And they're surprising high in calories, which is always a plus in a survival situation.

Ramen noodles are meant to be eaten as a soup. But try them dry some time. We have them for dinner all the time, as a side dish instead of potatoes or macaroni and cheese. Just boil them, drain them, and then add the seasonings. Stir well and serve.

In a survival situation, you can feed your team five packs of Ramen noodles a day. That's 1900 calories, which will keep them going. And it costs seventy cents per man per day. How much were those MREs again?

Another reason I like the Ramen noodles is because they're so filling. If you eat those five packages a day, you're stuffed. You're not looking around for something else to eat. So it helps your mental outlook as well.

We've got stacks and stacks of Ramen noodles in an extra bedroom in our house. And I'm not worried about them going bad. They'll outlive you and me and our grandkids.

Something else I want you to store a lot of is coffee and hot cocoa, and for several reasons.

I know coffee isn't cheap these days. But in my household it's pretty much essential to life. Sarah and I are both people who have had three or four cups a day for most of our lives.

After doomsday hits, coffee will be our only vice. We're not stocking any alcohol, except for a bottle if whisky we're saving to sterilize wounds (yes, like in old *Gunsmoke* episodes where Doc pours whiskey on a wound to sterilize it, it does indeed work in a pinch. It burns more than a hooker has crabs, but it works).

It isn't that we have anything against alcohol on religious grounds or anything. It's just that it's so damn expensive.

I know, I know, some of the books you've read on prepping say you should hoard alcohol because you can barter with it later on.

And that's true, if you have the money to hoard alcohol. We're on a budget. If we hoard alcohol, that's less money we'll have to hoard food. We can always barter with food too, and food will keep you alive. Alcohol won't.

Same with cigarettes.

I don't smoke, neither does Sarah. And we don't judge people who do. It's a personal decision. Our friend Cinda doesn't smoke, but her husband Tim does. Cinda's been trying to get him to quit for years, but he hasn't been able to. He's said lately that he'll quit when and if the apocalypse makes him quit, and not before.

His plan is to always keep two full cartons of cigarettes at home. Every time he opens one of them, he'll get another one to replace it.

He says that when doomsday happens, he'll have two cartons of cigarettes to help him wean himself off of them. And hopefully by cutting back and only smoking when he has to, that he'll feel no pain when he's out.

He's a good guy. I hope that works for him.

Anyway, we know that if doomsday keeps us sheltered in place for any length of time, that alcohol and tobacco won't be available. But coffee will be because we'll make sure we stock enough for awhile. We'll also have some unroasted coffee beans. Cinda says she's not sure she'll be able to get them to grow, but she's willing to try.

We view coffee as almost an essential, for several reasons. First of all, it'll be a morale booster. Nothing gets you out of bed on a cold day faster than the smell of fresh coffee brewing.

Also, it's going to be a nice treat, of sorts, in a world in which damn few treats will exist.

By the way, this is kind of off the track a bit, but coffee makes it a lot easier to eat hard tack and enjoy it. Dipping it in hot coffee softens it and makes it easier to chew. And then it's not so bland because it tastes like coffee…

And last, it will help prevent dehydration. We know we have to drink a certain amount of water to keep our organs functioning properly and to stay on our toes. When it's thirty degrees inside your house because the power grid's down and you're conserving generator fuel, there's nothing appetizing or endearing about ice cold water. So we tend to drink less of it.

On the other hand, announce that there's fresh hot coffee when it's thirty degrees, and people will line up for it.

Hot cocoa is kinda the same thing, only with the added benefit of being very high in calories and capable of satisfying one's sweet tooth. We don't count hot cocoa calories on the white board tally in the garage, so it's a freebie. But it does indeed augment the calories we do count, and it'll help keep our family happy and healthy.

So it's kinda win-win.

Peanut butter and jelly sandwiches are win-win too. We stock a lot of peanut butter and jelly.

Our jelly is always in glass jars, so that we can dip the top of the jar in melted wax and extend its shelf life. Peanut better doesn't really go bad, but it does dry out over time. You can fix that just by pouring a little bit of vegetable oil in and stirring it.

Even in the dead of winter, a cold peanut butter and jelly sandwich is pretty darn good. It's relatively high in calories, so it doesn't take too many sandwiches to give everyone their daily calorie goal. And everybody likes them.

In the winter, put them in zip lock bags and pass them out. Have your people put them inside their coats, and drop them into their coat sleeves. After an hour they'll be soft and warm and will taste much better.

Serving PBJs in the winter will also stretch your fuel, which is particularly important if you're running low on it and it's a while before spring comes around and you can replenish it.

And peanut butter and jelly sandwiches, whether it's spring or summer, will boost everybody's morale by providing them a rare treat in a harsh world.

The whole secret behind storing food on a budget is not to get too fancy. I've seen prepping shows where fat women who are used to eating crab legs and caviar are stocking fancy foo-foo food and spending a fortune for it.

But I don't have that kind of money. What I do have is a desire to keep my family alive, and an imagination to make it happen. And if we have to eat Ramen noodles every day for a month, so what? We'll be just as alive in the end as the fat lady. And we'll still be around, when most of the rest of the world has starved to death because they weren't smart enough to prepare.

Many of you were in the military, like me. You've been in the field, and you've had nasty food in portable field kitchens or old fashioned c-rations or MREs.

Many others of you grew up like I did. I grew up in a poor household. My father was a carefree sort in his early years, and frequently did very dumb things like quitting jobs because he didn't like his boss.

Back then, mothers stayed home and didn't work. There were times when my mother took in ironing, or babysat other women's children to help pay the bills, but there was only so much she could do.

There were many times when I was a kid when I went to bed hungry at night.

And whether you grew up as I did, or ate the same kind of foods I did in the military, you and I know the truth about food that others don't know.

Food is fuel. That's all it is. Sure, it's nice when it tastes yummy and there's a wide variety. But when it's not so tasty or so plentiful, it's still food. It still does the trick.

Tell those people who whine about the food to suck it up, buttercup. The alternative is starving to death. And there will be plenty of other people doing that.

Given a choice, I choose survival. Everything else is small potatoes.

Thank you for reading
The Final Days of the United States
And How You Can Survive Them

I hope you found the information helpful and can put it to good use.

Prepping is like football, You can discuss it for months, and you haven't even made a dent. There's always more to talk about.

The Final Days of the United States And How You Can Survive Them Book 2 will be available in September, 2018 from Amazon.com and through Barnes and Noble.

In *Book 2,* we'll talk about how to build a Faraday cage to protect your electronic items and generator from EMPs. We'll talk about which items to include, and how to tell how many items you can run off your generator at the same time.

We'll discuss how to collect fuel to run your generator, and even give you an option for a separate source of power if your generator ever goes out or you don't have one.

We'll talk about how to get your vehicle running again, after solar generated EMPs have shorted out all the vehicles in your area.

We'll discuss emergency evacuation procedures and how to establish a safe house close by in the event you're ever overrun.

And we'll begin to discuss life after the apocalypse. How to exit your compound for the first time when the world starts getting back to normal. How to deal with your neighbors that are still alive.

We'll talk about how to raise your crops. How to safely go on resupply runs to gather the things you need but don't have.

If the need calls for banding together with your neighborhood for mutual protection, we'll talk about tips to help you get through it.

We'll discuss more of my favorite subject: food, and more tips on how to prepare and store it.

And how to barter without being shot.

And one of the big things we'll talk about is something a lot of preppers have never even considered: your plan for gathering your family members or team members, who may be spread out all over town, if an EMP strikes and all the vehicles stop working.

Again, we don't what will happen in the coming years that will cause a doomsday situation. My own personal belief, based on things I've read and studied, is that solar storms and EMPs are the most likely scenario. I just have a gut feeling that's what we'll have to deal with.

We know what they say about opinions, though, and your opinion about what the future holds is just as valid as mine.

But here's the deal. As preppers, we're not limited to plan for just one scenario. It makes sense to plan for as many as we can. And to have contingency plans that we can put into place no matter what curve balls are thrown our way.

And we'll throw in other miscellaneous tips that will make things go a lot easier for you and your family or group emotionally and psychologically, when that time comes we're all dreading.

And make it easier you to survive it.

Good luck in your prepping. See you in *Book 2*.

-Charlie-

****

Please enjoy this preview of
**The Final Days of the United States
And How You Can Survive Them
Book 2**

****

Each person in your group will need at least one sleeping bag. Two would be a lot better, if you live in a part of the country where temperatures drop below freezing. And if you live in the upper third of the country, the second sleeping bag should be considered mandatory.

Depending on the winter temperatures in your area, your people might be able to get by with just a double winter bag. On the box it'll say "two person sleeping bag." The only way you can fit two normal sized people inside this bag comfortably is to stack them on top of each other. Which might not be a bad thing, depending on the people. Remember, these are made by the same company that makes tents with six square feet of floor space and calls it a "four man tent."

They obviously use midgets or children to measure their products.

Anyway, although the two person bag isn't big enough for two people, it will accommodate one normal sized person with room to spare. That's good, because your people aren't going to sleep alone.

You're going to all learn to wash up and change clothes in a sleeping bag.

No, I'm not crazy. It's a standard practice for winter campers. When you wake up in the morning, it'll be a hell of a lot warmer in the bag than outside of it. You're not going to want to crawl out of your bag, take off your clothes when it's twenty degrees, and put on clothes that have been outside the bag all night long and are also twenty degrees.

No. What you're going to do is put your change of clothes inside the bag with you when you go to bed at night. They won't be body temperature the next morning, but they'll be close. And because you've got some extra room in this larger bag, you can move around (wiggle and squirm, Sarah calls it).

Inside the bag, you can remove your dirty clothing. Toss it outside the bag where it's out of your way. Then feel around for your clean clothing. For some reason, it's almost always down by your feet or underneath your body. But that's okay. Because those are the two warmest parts of the bag, and they'll feel a lot better when you put them on.

But wait, you're not finished yet. You have to clean your body. You can't shower or wash in a sink, but you can use baby wipes. The ones that come in a canister, not a brick. I'll explain why in a bit.

Use the baby wipes to wipe down the strategic parts of your body. You know which ones. They're the only parts you really wash when you're in the shower.

And go a step farther. Wash your feet. Especially between your toes. You can and will get trench foot, even in the wintertime, if you make no effort to keep your feet clean.

I know what you're thinking. You won't have enough clean clothes to change daily. And that's true. But that doesn't mean you can't make the effort occasionally to clean your body. Whether it's once a day or once a week, it's still important.

After you wash your body, apply deodorant and get dressed. The baby wipes and deodorant will stay in the bag all winter long, so they'll be reasonably warm when you use them.

And there are other things you can put in your bag as well. If you're in an environment where you have frequent winter storms, or very low temperatures, it may not go above freezing for several days at a time. You obviously cannot drink frozen water.

But you can keep your own personal water supply, in the form of several small bottles of drinking water, inside your sleeping bag. Your body heat will help it thaw at night, and you can place it on the *inside* of your coat to keep it thawed during the day.

Three more things about this.

Many preppers make a mistake by hoarding only food and water. It never occurs to them to hoard other things as well. Like, for example, laundry soap, baby wipes and deodorant.

Yes, I know, things like that are not absolutely essential to survival.

But they are indeed essential to surviving with any semblance of normalcy and self respect.

I said earlier to buy the baby wipes that come in a canister, instead of a brick. There are two reasons for this. They are more air tight. The wipes are less likely to dry out. And it they do, you can just pop the top off he canister and pour a quarter cup of water inside to moisten them again. Try doing that with a brick and you'll just make a mess.

We'll talk later about how to hoard things like baby wipes and deodorant to make them last for three years or more.

If you live in a northern or very cold climate, the second sleeping bag is essential. Here's why:

Depending on the brand of winter sleeping bags you buy, the first bag will keep you warm in temperatures down to twenty to thirty degrees. But a second winter bag, placed inside the first, will keep you toasty warm even when the temperatures drop way below zero.

The second bag needs to be a regular size bag. Sleep on one side of the big bag, and keep the small bag's zipper on the inside of the big bag. That way you'll have plenty of spare room to store your stuff without putting it in the smaller bag, where it may get in your way. And, you can unzip the small bag in the morning to give you more room to get dressed.

I know, winter sleeping bags are expensive. But you don't have to buy them all at once. We bought one per payday over the course of several months.

And remember, if you know a single person at work or in the neighborhood who's a prepper, you can always offer him a chance to buy in.

I talked about this a little in my first book, but if you missed it, here's the deal. A single guy in a big bad world will be a sitting duck for gangs of marauders.

But you'll have a safe place to hide in plain sight, and a security system that will keep you safe.

Assuming this guy isn't somebody you just can't stand, offer him a chance to buy his way in. Tell him he has to purchase sleeping bags for the entire group, and hoard three years' worth of food to bring in with him.

On the face of it, this may appear a little bit shady. It may appear (or he may think) that you're taking advantage of him.

But explain to him the bigger picture. It's actually a win win situation. The food is for him if he wants to eat his own provisions. Or, he can add it to the pile and eat with everybody else. And he'd have to hoard the food even if he wasn't joining your group.

In exchange for the sleeping bags, tell him he gets a security system that will watch out for bad guys even when he's sleeping. He'll have the strength of numbers if you ever do battle with anyone. And he'll have people to administer first aid to him if he's ever hurt or wounded.

There will be others to help do chores like keeping a fire going and gathering wood and fuel and water.

Plus, the camaraderie of being in a group will keep him from going crazy.

Like I said, you're not taking advantage of him. You're helping him as much as he's helping you.

One last thing regarding the sleeping bags. Some stores may not have the shelf space to accommodate winter sleeping bags in the summertime.

If that's the case, you *must* resist the urge to say, "Well, the summer sleeping bag will have to do…"

I can't express this enough. A summer sleeping bag is worthless to you. It's little more than a thin blanket with a zipper, and in a harsh winter you can freeze to death inside of it.

You can buy winter bags all year around on the internet. Amazon.com has some good deals on winter bags in the summer. So does Academy Sports and Walmart.com

As for the summer time when it's hot, you still don't need a lighter bag. All you have to do is strip down to your shorts and a t-shirt and sleep on top of the winter bag.

www.ingramcontent.com/pod-product-compliance
Lightning Source LLC
Chambersburg PA
CBHW060618290526
45793CB00001B/70